W9-AAL-494

CHURCHES OF
Nova Scotia

CHURCHES OF
Nova Scotia

Robert Tuck

with photographs by Graham Tuck

THE DUNDURN GROUP
TORONTO

Copyright © Robert Tuck, 2004

All rights reserved. No part of this publication may be reproduced, stored in a retrieval system, or transmitted in any form or by any means, electronic, mechanical, photocopying, recording, or otherwise (except for brief passages for purposes of review) without the prior permission of Dundurn Press. Permission to photocopy should be requested from Access Copyright.

Copy-Editor: Michael Hodge
Design: Jennifer Scott
Printer: Transcontinental

National Library of Canada Cataloguing in Publication Data

Tuck, Robert
    Churches of Nova Scotia / Robert Tuck.

Includes bibliographical references.
ISBN 1-55002-478-7

1. Church buildings — Nova Scotia — History. 2. Church architecture — Nova Scotia — History. I. Title.

NA5246.N6T82 2003   726'.5'09716   C2003-904047-X

1   2   3   4   5   08   07   06   05   04

We acknowledge the support of the **Canada Council for the Arts** and the **Ontario Arts Council** for our publishing program. We also acknowledge the financial support of the **Government of Canada** through the **Book Publishing Industry Development Program** and **The Association for the Export of Canadian Books**, and the **Government of Ontario** through the **Ontario Book Publishers Tax Credit** program, and the **Ontario Media Development Corporation's Ontario Book Initiative.**

Care has been taken to trace the ownership of copyright material used in this book. The author and the publisher welcome any information enabling them to rectify any references or credit in subsequent editions.
                    J. Kirk Howard, President

Printed and bound in Canada.✪
Printed on recycled paper.

www.dundurn.com

Dundurn Press	Gazelle Book Services Limited	Dundurn Press
8 Market Street	White Cross Mills	2250 Military Road
Suite 200	Hightown, Lancaster, England	Tonawanda NY
Toronto, Ontario, Canada	LA1 4X5	U.S.A. 14150
M5E 1M6		

To Catherine Elizabeth Greene,
Church Youth Worker in Nova Scotia 1954–58

Photo by Graham Tuck

Christ as The Good Shepherd — an altarpiece by Robert Harris, 1849–1919, from Trinity Church, Sydney Mines.

Table of Contents

Introduction

THE BUILDING OF CHURCHES FIRST got underway as a major human activity in the fourth century after the so-called Edict of Milan in 313 enabled Christians in the Roman world to emerge from hidden refuges and practise their religion openly. The architectural idiom they chose to use was not that of the classical temple associated with pagan religion but that of the basilica, or secular government assembly building. Generally speaking, a basilica consisted of a rectangular hall, or nave, sometimes flanked by lower-roofed aisles, or wings, from which its central space was divided by arcades of piers with a line of clerestory windows above, under a flat ceiling. At one end was a rounded apse in which the magistrate had his chair. This spot was adopted by the Christians for placement of the altar, and behind it was the chair of the celebrant, who presided at the celebration of the Eucharist, or the thanksgiving for Christ and his sacrifice, the principal act of Christian worship. If the celebrant was a bishop, or overseer, the chair was his cathedra, and the building a cathedral. Sometimes, if the church had been erected over the burial place of a martyr or an apostle, or if it marked a holy site, there was an opening in the floor in front of the altar through which worshippers might access the site, or reliquary, that contained the bones of the saint. This is how the great churches were ordered that marked the places of Christ's Nativity and Resurrection in the Holy Land, as well as those that celebrated the witness of apostles and saints in Rome and elsewhere across North Africa, the Middle East, and Europe.

The European settlers who came to Nova Scotia in the seventeenth and eighteenth centuries thus were heirs to a history and tradition of church-building that extended back more than a thousand years. The extent to which what they built and how they went about building it differed from that to which they had been accustomed in their motherlands was determined partly by the materials for building available in Nova Scotia and partly by local differences in climate and social conditions. Thus when the earliest still-standing church building in Nova Scotia, St. Paul's in Halifax, was built in the neo-Classical style in imitation of St. Peter's, Vere Street, in London, it was unlike St. Peter's in that it was made of wood rather than of brick and stone. Its timbers were prefabricated in Boston, Massachusetts, and shipped to Nova Scotia for assembly in Halifax.

In England, there was a sharp social distinction between the established Church of England and the so-called free or nonconformist or dissenting places of worship. The nonconformist buildings were called chapels rather than churches, and — like the early Christian basilicas — were built to look like secular rather than religious buildings. Indeed, the Reverend John Wesley, founder of the Methodists, who was a priest of the Church of England, was careful to design his movement as a society within the church, rather than as a church in competition with the Church of England. This was reflected in the architecture of Methodism's chapels, which looked much more like village meeting halls than they did like churches. It was not until after Wesley's death in 1791 that the Methodists, in 1795, took the step of authorizing their preachers to perform ministerial functions even though they were without any form of ordination. But Wesley and his associates many years before had been rebuffed by the bishops and denied the use of the parish churches for their meetings. In this the bishops — largely latitudinarian (or as we would say today, liberal) in their theology — proved to be far less imaginative and open-minded than Pope Innocent III was in the thirteenth century when he welcomed that era's equivalent of John Wesley, Saint Francis of Assisi, and gave him his blessing, guidance, and support. So it was that in the early colonial period in Nova Scotia, as elsewhere across the English-speaking world, the established church tended to be left high

and dry while the Holy Spirit moved outside its boundaries to win souls to Christ. In Nova Scotia we see this difference between church and chapel expressed in the architectural differences between St. Paul's Church and the Inglis-era churches on the one hand, and buildings like the Barrington Meeting House and the Grand Pré Covenanters' Church on the other — although we must be clear that these particular buildings predate Methodism, and their lineage is Congregationalist. But it did not last long, and just as the Methodists in England started ordaining ministers with the laying on of hands in 1836, so too over time the meeting houses of Methodists and other nonconformist bodies became churches with ecclesiastical appurtenances like steeples that made them almost indistinguishable from Anglican buildings, at least in their exterior appearance. An example of this process is the Covenanter Church at Grand Pré, a meeting-house-style building erected in 1804. It was built by the mostly Congregationalist New England planters — under Scottish Presbyterian leadership — who had been settled on the Grand Pré lands vacated by Acadians expelled by the British military in 1755. Architecturally, it was transformed into a church, at least in its exterior appearance, by the addition of a steeple in 1818.

The situation of the Roman Catholic churches was different. The Roman Catholics in British-ruled territories like Nova Scotia were similar to the New England Congregationalists and the old-country Methodists in that they were religious nonconformists who did not accept the church established by law, the United Church of England and Ireland. Just as Roman Catholic clergy were inhibited by law from appearing in public in clerical garb, so too their chapels tended to look unlike churches in their exterior appearance, often lacking steeples, for example. But if the Catholics were Acadian French who had evaded expulsion, or Highland Scots who had not been embraced by Presbyterianism, or newly arrived immigrant Irish, they represented the pre-Reformation or Counter-Reformation Catholic religious tradition that Protestantism sought to change. The British had been at war, on and off, with the French for centuries, but this was only part of the reason why, at the time Nova Scotia was founded, and for almost two hundred years before that, Roman Catholics in places under British rule were severely restricted in respect to the free exercise of not only their religion but also their civil rights. These disabilities had their origins in the unresolved religious conflicts of the sixteenth century that divided Europeans into Reformation and Counter-Reformation camps. In 1570, Pope Pius V had excommunicated the Queen of England, Elizabeth I, and absolved her subjects of their allegiance to her. This had the unfortunate effect of making Roman Catholicism equivalent to treason in places where the English crown was sovereign, and in England after 1570 the persecution of Catholics began to approach in severity that of an earlier persecution of Protestants by Elizabeth's half-sister, the Roman Catholic Queen Mary, who burned more than three hundred Protestants alive in the six years she was Queen of England, from 1552 to 1558. The crucial role played by Mary in the creation of anti-Catholic sentiment in the Anglo-Saxon world often goes unnoticed because the attention of historical memory has been much more focussed on the colourful but brutal father she shared with Elizabeth, King Henry VIII. When Mary became Queen on

the death of their half-brother, Edward VI, most people in England had been alienated from Protestant reform by the vandalism and bigotry that had accompanied its imposition by Edward's ministers, and they not altogether unwillingly accepted the restoration of papal authority over the Church of England that was ordered by Mary, using the powers inherent in the title concocted by Henry for himself, Head of the Church of England, that Mary had inherited. Unfortunately, Mary set out to punish those whom she saw as responsible for the ill-treatment that had been accorded her mother, Henry's admirable first wife, Queen Catherine of Aragon, and she embarked on a vicious program of burning Protestants at the stake. Contemporary observers, and others since, have found it difficult to feel much sympathy for some of the Protestant victims, like bishops Latimer and Ridley, who seemed rather to enjoy being burned alive;[1] but when the tremulous old Archbishop of Canterbury, Thomas Cranmer, author of the Book of Common Prayer, was consigned to the flames in the middle of the street in the city of Oxford at a spot now marked by a cross set in the cobblestones (today irreverently known as the Cranmer Hot Spot), a wave of revulsion swept across England. It was clear that religion had gotten out of hand, and Elizabeth, on ascending the throne in 1558, in attempting to control and pacify religious passions, nationalized the church, in much the same way governments have nationalized various things like railways and health care in modern times. It was when it became clear that Elizabeth's policy was having some success, and that a second restoration of papal authority over the English church was increasingly unlikely, that the pope, in 1570, issued his decree deposing the queen that led to the consequent persecution of Catholics. The late Queen Mary's husband, Philip II, the "Most Catholic" King of Spain, attempted to enforce the papal decree by sending an Armada against England in 1588 after Elizabeth had reluctantly ordered Mary Queen of Scots (in the Roman Catholic view the rightful queen of England) beheaded in 1587. The Armada failed, but the ill-humour and mutual fears of the successors of these protagonists continued to be reflected in the laws and behaviours that marked the relationships of their successors in Nova Scotia (and elsewhere) in the late eighteenth century and even into recent times.

In the view of British government and governors, the established church was a bulwark not only against papal authoritarianism on the one hand and irrational enthusiasm and fanaticism in religion on the other, but also against novel and upsetting ideas about how society should be organized and how people should live in it. In the late eigh-

Bishop Charles Inglis's well at Clermont. The inscription on the plaque reads: "This is the site of CLERMONT, the estate of CHARLES INGLIS, who was consecrated the first Anglican Bishop of Nova Scotia in 1787. He purchased this land in 1790 and had this well dug in 1792. He died here on Feb. 24th, 1816."

Photo by Graham Tuck

teenth and early nineteenth centuries, republicanism — as bred in France and established in the United States — and lunatic fringes of anarchists and levellers were viewed very much as political and religious fundamentalists of various left- and right-wing persuasions are today. It requires some exercise of historical imagination now to stroll about inside a lovely old meeting house, with its antique window glass and the reeded panels on its old pine box pews, and realize that two hundred years ago many of the people in the pretty Georgian-Style Anglican church a few miles down the road, sitting under the three-decker pulpit and warming their feet on hot bricks listening to hour-long sermons denouncing the Philistines, regarded those worshipping in the meeting house as dangerous incipient republican agitators who could set cities on fire and drive comfortably-off people like themselves into the woods in ox carts. But that is exactly what had happened just a few years before in New York as that old Irishman, Bishop Charles Inglis, who had been rector of Trinity Church in New York throughout the American rebellion, and had faced down George Washington's muskets levelled at him from the front pews as he prayed for God's blessing on His Majesty King George, could testify. Afterwards Inglis had fled with his fellow Loyalists, and in England had been consecrated Bishop for the established church in what remained of British North America under the title Bishop of Nova Scotia. In his declining years he kept pretty much to his rural retreat at Clermont, near Aylesford, in the Annapolis Valley. He had lived through it all, and had found it immensely distressing. It must never happen again! God save the king — and us! — from the twin mischiefs of republicanism in the state and enthusiasm in religion!

Chapter One
Saint Paul's, Halifax:
Victorian Georgian

WHEN BISHOP CHARLES INGLIS SET foot ashore in Halifax on October 17, 1787, St. Paul's Church (erected on the Grand Parade the year after the founding of the city in 1749) became, in effect, St. Paul's Cathedral, for it was there that Inglis had his episcopal chair, or cathedra. A few weeks later, on November 25, the members of the Nova Scotia Legislative Assembly attended St. Paul's in a body so that the bishop might preach to them. Twenty-nine years before, in 1758, the assembly had declared the Church of England to be the established church of Nova Scotia, even though it commanded the allegiance of a minority of the population of the colony. Inglis's jurisdictions as bishop were defined in two royal patents: by one he was bishop of the diocese of Nova Scotia "and its dependencies" for life; by the other he had episcopal jurisdiction in the other British North America colonies and territories "at the Royal pleasure," that is, until they too should be erected into dioceses with their own bishops.[2]

The St. Paul's Church in which Charles Inglis addressed the assembly differed considerably from the building familiar to Haligonians today, especially in its exterior appearance. In 1787 St. Paul's was a rectangular box, ninety feet long by fifty-six feet wide, in the Georgian style, closely patterned on James Gibbs's St. Peter's Church, Vere Street, in the city of London, the plans for which had been published some years earlier and so were readily available. It was placed with its end elevations oriented north and south at the narrow south end of a rectangular square called the Grand Parade, set in the centre of the grid of streets that constituted Halifax.

In 1787 St. Paul's was still very much as it had been built — or assembled, for its constituent timbers had been pre-fabricated in New England — in 1750. The site on which it stood was steep, sloping sharply upwards from the harbour to the hilltop that rose above the mostly flat plateau of the Halifax peninsula. The Grand Parade in 1787 was still just a bare patch of cleared ground on the slope of the hillside, for it was not excavated and levelled until 1796. Each side elevation of the church building accommodated two rows of seven round-headed windows, the upper range almost

A view of Halifax c. 1763, showing Government House and St. Matthew's (Mather's) Church on Hollis Street, and looking up George Street to St. Paul's Church; oil on canvas by Dominique Serres, working from a drawing made by a military artist using a Camera Obscura.

Courtesy of the Art Gallery of Nova Scotia

twice the height of the lower. In the centre of the north end elevation was what is commonly called a Palladian window, flanked by two pairs of windows identical to those in the east and west elevations. Set in the centre of the elevation under the Palladian window was an entry porch in which the door was flanked by double columns that supported a triangular pediment that was repeated in the gable of the building. The south end elevation was identical to that of the north except that there was no entrance under the Palladian window and the two lower-range windows of the other facade were replaced by two square-headed doorways, each surmounted by a bracketed cornice and approached by a flight of steps, four to the upper door and five to the one lower down. Set within each of the pedimented gables was a round window, or oculus, that provided light to the attic space between ceiling and roof. The corners of the building and the window surrounds were ornamented by wooden quoins that attempted to convey the impression of stone construction. The glass in the multi-mullioned windows was small paned.

Inside, galleries ran the full length of the building and across its back. At the front, below the Palladian window, a small Communion table was enclosed by a rail. The earliest photograph of the interior of the church dates from c.1859–68 and shows a high "wineglass" pulpit reached by a narrow, curved, cast iron stair set off-centre in the middle of the central nave alley; but a description of the church as it had been prior to the middle of the century, published in the *Halifax Mail* in 1893, suggested that there had been an earlier and different layout and arrangement of the sanctuary furniture:

> The Communion Table stood against the southern wall, with a low railing before it. The pulpit — a three-decker — was a little to the west of the central aisle. On either side — east and west — were square pews for the officers of the army and navy. On either side of the centre aisle, in front of the Communion Table, were the pews for the Governor, the Admiral and the Bishop. The Governor's pew was a miniature drawing room. It was square, luxuriously furnished with tables, a desk, chairs, etc. The Admiral's pew was equally comfortable. Both were upholstered in crimson. The Bishop's pew was upholstered in blue.

Set saddleback on the crest of the roof over the entrance front was a squat, four-sided tower surmounted by two octagonal cupolas, one smaller than and set above the other, each with round-headed, louvered, full-length windows in each of its eight bays. It was topped by a weathervane.

The construction of St. Paul's was rapid (no doubt assisted by the prefabrication), and the first service in it was offered on September 2, 1750, less than three months after Governor Edward Cornwallis laid its cornerstone on June 13. Yet for the next twelve years the church is described only as "almost finished" in letters and various other written references.[3] Finally, in a letter dated February 27, 1763, its rector, the Reverend John Breynton, describes it as "now compleatly finished and will (when our organ is erected) be the neatest in North America..."

As the years passed, and the eighteenth century gave way to the nineteenth, St. Paul's received the usual maintenance required by a wooden building in an exposed position in a harsh climate. The original imitation quoins around the windows were replaced by simpler surrounds, and those on the corners of the building by the wide pilasters common in late eighteenth and early nineteenth century wooden buildings in the Maritime provinces. The building was painted from time to time, usually in an off-white or cream colour, later "stone colour" or grey. The earliest photograph of St. Paul's, made in 1853, suggests that it was at that time grey with white trim.

The first major change in the building came in 1812, when a large vestibule, or narthex, flanked by two vestries was constructed on the elevation facing the Parade. The old steeple, which had become dilapidated, was taken down, and a replica erected on the new extension. In the early years of the nineteenth century there was an open gallery, rather like a veranda, on the south end elevation below the Palladian window that linked the two exterior doors. This was a curious structure, the appearance of which seems never to have been recorded in any visual form. It appears to have been used to stage entertainments such as boxing matches!

In 1868 the church was enlarged by the addition of aisles, or wings, on the east and west sides of the nave, providing seating for an additional two hundred persons and increasing the width of the building from fifty-six to eighty feet. The old lower ranges of windows were discarded, and new, two-light, sashed, Romanesque-style windows with rounded heads were installed. This led to the replacement the next year of the old upper range of windows by new ones made in similar style to those below, but with a roundel set at the top between the two vertical lights.

Four years later, a chancel twenty-eight feet deep with flanking vestries was built on the southern end of the church. The old Palladian window was replaced by a massive three-light Romanesque-style window that incorporated two roundels with quatrefoil tracery in its head. All the detailing was derived from Classical originals, but the spirit of the changes was Gothic Revival, which by the 1860s had become the dominant architectural idiom in the Anglo-Saxon world. St. Paul's, as originally built, had closely resembled St. Peter's, Vere Street, on the outside; but now it looked very little like St. Peter's even in its exterior. Traces of its character as an eighteenth-century Georgian building survived in spots, but now, for the most part, St. Paul's had been transformed into a Victorian

building, both inside and out, with Italianate and Gothic-Revival influences evident in its new chancel layout, furniture, and fenestration.

This enlargement of the building, and its updating, took place shortly after the fourth Bishop of Nova Scotia, Hibbert Binney, had moved his episcopal chair from St. Paul's in 1864 to St. Luke's, a Gothic-Revival-style wooden building that stood on Morris Street in the south end of the city, which now became the diocesan pro-cathedral. Binney was a Tractarian, an advocate of the Catholic Revival in the Anglican Church, and, as such, he was regarded with suspicion by more Protestant-minded Anglicans. When he wanted to place a credence table in the sanctuary at St. Paul's on which to place the Eucharistic bread and wine until it should be needed on the holy table for consecration as the Body and Blood of Christ, there was an uproar when his request was refused. The bishop moved his chair out of St. Paul's, which then reverted to its original status as a parish church, to St. Luke's.

An earlier dispute was more serious. When Bishop Charles Inglis died, aged eighty-one, in 1816, the diocese of Nova Scotia had been run for some time by his son, the Reverend John Inglis, rector of St. Mary's Church, Aylesford, as his father's commissary. In those days, and for many more to come, no provision was made for clergy pensions, and in consequence, the clergy seldom retired. In 1808, and again in 1812, Charles had attempted to get the British government to authorize John's consecration as his suffragan, or as coadjutor bishop, but without success. After Bishop Charles was laid to rest under St. Paul's Church, John sailed for England, expecting that he might return as bishop; but on the same ship,

Photo by Graham Tuck

St. Paul's Church, Halifax, 1750: exterior from The Grand Parade.

unknown to John, was a memorandum signed by some of the leading citizens of Halifax requesting that the rector of St. Paul's, the Reverend Robert Stanser, be consecrated bishop of Nova Scotia. So it was that John Inglis returned to Nova Scotia not as bishop, but as rector of St. Paul's, with Stanser now his bishop in the place of his late father.

But Stanser returned to England within two years, where he continued to draw his salary *in absentia* for eight more years, while John Inglis performed as commissary for Stanser, as he had for his aged father. Stanser was eventually persuaded to resign by the promise of a pension, and John Inglis was at last consecrated bishop of Nova Scotia

Photo by Graham Tuck

St. Paul's Church, Halifax: interior.

by the archbishop of Canterbury in Lambeth Palace Chapel on Palm Sunday, 1825.

This meant, of course, that a new rector would have to be found for St. Paul's. John Inglis had left the parish in charge of his curate, the Reverend John Thomas Twining. As soon as word reached Halifax that John Inglis was to be the new bishop, Twining asked the churchwardens to call a meeting to recommend his appointment to the "highly respectable and responsible position" of rector of St. Paul's.[4] This they did; but not long afterwards they received a letter from John Inglis telling them that the appointment lay with the Crown rather than with the parishioners, and that the Reverend Robert Willis of Saint John, New Brunswick, not Mr. Twining, had been appointed rector of St. Paul's. Push came to shove in what was afterwards called the Great Disruption, and the churchwardens locked the church against Mr. Willis, whose induction, in consequence, took place outside the building. However, under the threat of legal action from the colonial secretary, a part of the congregation, including some leading families, withdrew from St. Paul's. They worshipped for a while in rented premises under Mr. Twining's leadership, and then he withdrew, having been offered an appointment as garrison chaplain. Some of them opted to attend St. George's Church on Brunswick Street, and the remaining dissidents, unable to find another Anglican priest who would minister to them, purchased a chapel on Granville Street and became Baptists. Their story is continued elsewhere in this book.

St. Paul's Church, Halifax.

Photo by R.C. Tuck.

St. Matthew's Church, Halifax: view from Old St. Paul's burying ground.

Chapter Two
St. Matthew's, Halifax:
Mather Church?

When Halifax was founded in 1749, it was peopled mostly with individuals rounded up in the poorer parts of London and shipped overseas to Nova Scotia. Within a very few years, many of them had perished from the cold, died in epidemics, or moved away. Their places were largely taken by a sharper and hardier sort of person from the Thirteen Colonies to the south, then still British subjects, attracted by the opportunities offered by the development taking place in Nova Scotia. Like the New England planters, who a little later on were settled on the lands from which the Acadians were expelled in 1755, they were, in religion, mostly dissenters from the established church of England, having learned their religion in Puritan congregations back home in New England. Before the end of 1749, Governor Cornwallis, in response to a request from the dissenters, gave four prime lots at the corner of Hollis and Prince streets that had been forfeited by their original proprietors (by reason of their failure to erect houses on them) as the site for a dissenters' chapel. Its construction began in 1753, and in 1754 the Governor's Council granted it £400. It was ready for use before the end of that year, and became known as Mather's Church.

But who was Mather? No one knows for sure. Thomas Raddall suggested that the chapel was named after Cotton Mather, the New England Puritan Divine, 1663–1728, famous for having presided at the celebrated witchcraft trials in Salem, Massachusetts — although he had been dead for a generation. Until their own building was ready, the dissenters used St. Paul's Church on the Grand Parade Sunday afternoons, their congregation consisting largely of the same persons who had already spent up to three hours at the Book of Common Prayer service of Morning Prayer and sermon at St. Paul's. The first minister of Mather's Church was the Reverend Aaron Cleveland, but after three years he left Halifax and went to England, where he took Holy Orders in the Church of England.

Perhaps Mather's Church was a nickname. Officially it was called The Protestant Dissenters' Church, but in popular parlance it continued to be called Mather's Church, as its renaming as the phonetically similar St. Matthew's

Photo by R.C. Tuck.

Model of Mather's Church, 1753.

the church dearly. Four years earlier the congregation had been granted by the Crown sixty-five acres west of Oxford Street in an area bounded by South Street and Jubilee Road, and running down to the Northwest Arm, to serve as glebe land, very much as St. Paul's Church had been given land in the north end of the city. On that Sunday a member of the navy and one of the military attended a service at the dissenters' church and heard Mr. Seccombe not only pray for the rebels' success in their war against the Crown, but also commend their cause to his congregation. Off they went and repeated what they'd heard to the authorities. The next day Seccombe was summoned to appear before the council and was charged with uttering treasonable thoughts. Three prominent citizens, Messrs. Salter, Fillis, and Smith, all members of the church, were also charged with treason. Happily, they and their minister were acquitted, for if found guilty in that day and age, and with a war on, they might well have been hanged. Seccombe was let off with a severe warning. But what really hurt was that the glebe land in the south end of the city that had been given to the church by the Crown was taken back and given to a senior military officer. In 1783, with the war over, the church requested its return. The request was refused, but the dissenters were offered instead an equivalent acreage of property in the vicinity of Armdale. Incredibly, they turned the offer down. After that, the authorities simply ignored the dissenters' church's requests for the return of the land it had been given and had lost — all because of a sermon.

After the American War of Independence, the Congregationalist element in the dissenters' church waned and the number of Presbyterians increased. There were dis-

Church in 1820 indicates. But by this time its congregation included a number of Presbyterians, and its early days as a Congregationalist stronghold with links to New England had faded.

Undoubtedly, the American Revolutionary War had something to do with this, for at that time, in the mid-1770s, the American rebels had sympathizers in the dissenters' congregation — none more so than their minister, the Reverend John Seccombe. His expression of support for the Americans one Sunday in the summer of 1775 cost

Photo by R.C. Tuck.

St. Matthew's Church, Halifax: interior.

putes between the two groups. The Congregationalists wanted ministers from New England, the Presbyterians ministers from Scotland; the Congregationalists wanted to sing hymns by Isaac Watts, the Presbyterians wanted to sing metrical psalms; the Congregationalists wanted Communion four times a year, the Presbyterians just once. According to historian Dr. Will R. Bird, the struggle between the two groups lasted three years until a settlement was reached and an agreement signed on January 16, 1787, under the terms of which the Congregationalists got the quarterly Communion and the hymn-singing they wanted, and the Presbyterians the minister from Scotland.[5]

In the nineteenth century, temperance and Sabbath-observance became landmarks of Protestant religion, but in Halifax, at least, in the previous century some Protestants were more relaxed on these points than they were later on, as the tale of two Presbyterian elders, members of St. Matthew's, suggests. They were known to serve Communion in church Sunday mornings, and sell rum in their taverns Sunday afternoons. But this was before the rise and spread of Methodism that did so much to shape the attitudes of English-speaking populations in the Victorian era on both sides of the Atlantic.

St. Matthew's in the eighteenth century was much like other churches, in that it was unheated and its seating was at first scanty and then uncomfortable, with worship services dominated by long-winded sermons, during which people tended to nod off and fall asleep. Dr. Bird vividly describes the Protestant dissenters' church-going experience in Halifax in those early days:

> It was very cold in the church during the winter months as there was no heat whatever. The minister wore a long, heavy cloak over his regular attire, a heavy, lined hood and fur mittens. Men attending church were so bundled and wrapped with scarves they could barely walk in. Women wore seven petticoats, many shawls and capes and woolen gloves. The more wealthy had servants to carry in foot warmers made of iron and holding live coals. Others had heated bricks wrapped in blankets to supply warmth. Three women had fat poodles they brought to church and used as foot warmers. In 1795

fashions changed. Women wore but one petticoat, cotton hose instead of woollen, low shoes instead of ankle high laced footwear, and low-necked gowns. Women caught cold and died from chills taken in church. So a stove was installed on either side of the sanctuary and stoked the night before a service to heat the building. Services were very long. A sermon could last one and a half hours. Prayers lasted from forty minutes to an hour, and the congregation stood. An intermission was always given halfway through the prayer so that the infirm might sit and be rested.

There was no Garrison Chapel in Halifax for years and soldiers sat in the right of the gallery at St. Matthew's, the artillery and engineers on the left. As the artillery wore white starched trousers and blue jackets with long tails they made a fine appearance, but if the men were out late on Saturday night the long service was apt to make them sleepy. A Sergeant-major always stood in the centre of the gallery with a bug pole which he used to prod awake any unfortunate who started to snore. The best pews in St. Matthew's sold for $144.00 per year and were to the left and right of the sanctuary against the walls. Those next to them sold for $100.00 per year. In the centre were long benches without backs and these were free seats for the poor and for single women and men. Pew rents were paid quarterly and if payments were not on time the pew was auctioned. During the period from 1784 to 1850 all the leading business men of the town attended St. Matthew's and a man's credit in Halifax was judged by where he sat in the Church.

Morning service at St. Matthew's in the period 1784–1857 began at 9:00 am with a recital of the bills on hand asking for remembrances in prayers. A member might ask the congregation to pray for his wife or mother or child who was ailing. Another might ask for prayers on behalf of members of the family at sea, or prayers for a son or brother gone to the United States and not heard from. As the Bible chapter was read, it was explained verse by verse, and might take the better part of an hour. Afternoon service began at 2:00 pm and it was then that matters of offence were heard. The minister would read from the pulpit charges of slander. Mrs. White might accuse Mrs. Black of spreading false rumours, and would have witnesses to back her statements. Mrs. Black, if she had any hint of such proceedings would have her own witnesses. After slander cases came cases of debt. One member would name another who owed him but would not pay. Third were charges of flirtation. A wife would charge another of flirting with her husband. Last in the list were charges of drunkenness, and these were mostly made by the minister.[6]

In rural parts of Nova Scotia, the public recitation of sins by the sinners themselves was a feature of some Protestant revival services into the early years of the twentieth century, and provided not only an occasion for the sinners to come clean about their transgressions and receive an assurance of pardon, but also a source of inside information for those curious about their neighbours and their doings. Such services often attracted large congregations.

The old St. Matthew's Church burned on New Year's day in 1857, together with many other buildings in downtown Halifax. It was rebuilt on a new site (the present one) on Barrington Street, purchased from Bishop Binney, who lived nearby on the other side of Government House. The new St. Matthew's preserved the basic concept of the old building's meeting house interior layout, with a central pulpit in front of one end wall with galleries around the other three sides, but on the exterior it took the form of an elegant Gothic-Revival-style church with stucco finish and a buttressed tower surmounted by a slender spire. It was designed by Cyrus Thomas, 1833–1911, one of two architect sons of William Thomas, who designed the St. Lawrence Market and the Don Jail in Toronto. Cyrus was also the architect of the Halifax courthouse, just up the hill from St. Matthew's, on the opposite side of St. Paul's cemetery from the church. But the courthouse is in Classical, rather than Gothic, style; Thomas, like Stirling and some other architects of that era, used Gothic for ecclesiastical, and Classical style for civic and secular buildings.

Today, St. Matthew's takes pride in being the congregation of earliest foundation in the whole of the United Church of Canada.

Photo by Graham Tuck.

St. Mary's Church, Auburn.

Chapter Three
St. Mary's, Auburn:
Decency and Order

THE BUILDER OF ST. MARY'S Church, Auburn, Bishop Charles Inglis, was a native of Ireland who served United Church of England and Ireland parishes in Delaware and New York until his Loyalist sympathies alienated him in the United States after the American rebellion. When he arrived in Nova Scotia in 1787 as the newly consecrated first Anglican bishop in what was left of British North America, he was determined to see that everything in religion in the colony should be "done decently and in order," as St. Paul had counselled the Corinthians (1 Cor. 14:40). St. Mary's Church, built in 1790 in the neo-Classical Georgian style at Auburn in the heart of the Annapolis Valley, is very much the embodiment in architecture of decency and order.

However, at the end of the eighteenth century, and for some time thereafter, the religious scene in Nova Scotia was anything but orderly, and Inglis's "Anglican Design in Loyalist Nova Scotia" (as historian Judith Fingard calls it) fell some distance short of fulfillment.[7] It was a time when life for many was harsh and primitive, and enthusiasm (the word comes from the Greek *en theos*: "in God") in religion offered an excitement and release that the ordered cadences of the Anglican liturgy rather failed to provide. Nevertheless, over time decency and order made an impact, and although a majority of the colonists did not become Anglicans, their meeting houses became more and more like churches, with steeples and symbolism and eventually, in some cases, even a liturgical interior layout.

But Anglicanism itself was also subject to change, largely generated from within, in what is usually called the Tractarian Movement (from the tracts, or pamphlets, its members published to propagate their views). It began in the University of Oxford in England in 1833 with a sermon preached by the Reverend John Keble in which he argued that the established Church of England and Ireland was not a mere department of the state, but the ancient Church of the British Isles. It was a view that accorded well with the contemporary romantic fascination with the lore and legends of the Dark and Middle Ages, and the Gothic revival in architecture that accompanied it. As the nineteenth century proceeded, the Tractarian Movement produced changes not

St. Mary's Church, Auburn, 1790: exterior.

only in theology and liturgy, but also in the look of church buildings. Some of these changes can be traced in St. Mary's Church, and are evident also in many of the churches of all denominations in Nova Scotia. Indeed, our idea today of what a church looks like has been largely shaped by Tractarian and associated influences.

St. Mary's Church had a steeple and a liturgical layout inside from the start — although the interior today differs from that of 1790. The chancel then was shorter, consisting of little more than a small railed-in sanctuary accommodating only the holy table, or altar, and a pair of chairs set below a large Palladian-style window in the east wall. In front of it was

Photo by Graham Tuck.

St. Mary's Church, Auburn: interior. The panels on the end wall of the nave are of the Coat of Arms of the Diocese of Nova Scotia (left side) and King George III (right side), and are said to have been painted by Bishop Charles Inglis.

a three-decker pulpit, perhaps placed in the centre in front of the altar, but possibly on one side under the chancel arch. The parish clerk, who led the responses of the congregation, many of whom would not have been able to read, occupied the desk at the lowest level of the pulpit, while the minister sat above him to recite the divine office and read the lessons. The third level towered over them both, and was topped by a sounding board. It was occupied by the preacher during the sermon, which could go on for a long time. Many pulpits had an hourglass, which enabled the preacher to gauge the length of his oration, and he might turn it over once or twice in the course of his delivery if he was particularly long-winded. One of the nineteenth-century rectors of St. Mary's, the Reverend Richard Avery, whose thirty-three year incumbency, from 1852 to 1887, is the longest in the history of the parish, is recorded as always writing out his sermons in full "to make sure against saying anything in preaching that was not entirely correct" — yet it was he who, in 1856, took the three-decker pulpit apart, separating the clerk's desk from the rest of the structure.[8] This was the first impact the Tractarian Movement had on St. Mary's, for one of the goals of the Tractarians was to restore an even balance between Word and Sacrament in Anglican churches. Pulpit and lectern were no longer to dominate the altar, or preaching to overshadow the Holy Communion, as in the Georgian era with its enormous pulpits and celebrations of the Sacrament only once a quarter. Decency and order in Anglican worship now had to make room for the numinous as well. It was a shift that would have a profound effect on the architecture and appearance of churches.

The next things to go at St. Mary's were the box pews. The church was full of them, up a step from the floor of the alley that ran down the centre of the nave. Their sides were so high that when the worshippers sat down they could not see one another, and were visible only to the parson and the clerk in the pulpit. Each pew had its own door which, when shut, cut down draughts and kept in heat, for sometimes people brought hot bricks to church, and sometimes their dogs, on which to rest their feet in cold weather. Each pew at St. Mary's was numbered, and the pews were rented, thereby providing the parish with an important part of its income. Several pews were reserved: No. 1 was for "strangers," No. 16 for the bishop, No. 17 for members of the Rector's family, and No. 24 for "coloured people." Pew No. 9 was reserved for the Governor, but since his appearances at St. Mary's were infrequent it too was rented, on the understanding that its usual occupant would sit somewhere else when his excellency appeared. A pew was reserved for the bishop because Charles Inglis made his rural retreat, Clermont, a few miles west of Auburn, his principal residence after 1796.[9] About 1865, the sides of the box pews were lowered and given scroll-shaped tops, and their doors were removed. At the same time, the pew rents were abolished and anyone was free to sit anywhere they wished in the church.

Other changes involved the acquisition, in 1862, of a hand-pumped organ in a Gothic case, which was placed in the original part of the gallery at the west end of the nave (it had been extended in 1828 across the nave windows along both the north and south sides of the building). The gallery in Georgian churches normally accommodated singers and musical instruments as well as the occasional overflow congregation. But by the 1890s this arrangement for the placement of the singers and musicians seemed old-fashioned, for the new Gothic Revival churches then being built had extensive chancels, opening out from their naves and packed with choir stalls designed to accommodate the new, robed choirs that were being formed, whose members took delight in being seen as well as heard. It was a fashion that Canon Johnson of New York later described as "Cathedralesque Chancelitis."[10] So it was that, in 1891, St. Mary's small sanctuary was moved fifteen feet to the east. This placed it beyond the grave of Dr. Charles Inglis, the bishop's grandson, who had been buried just outside the church in 1861 and would, from now on, be under the floor as well as in the ground. Between the sanctuary and the nave, a chancel with choir stalls and organ alcove was created, the organ alcove on the south side balanced by a new sacristy on the north elevation. This gave St. Mary's a neo-Gothic layout, although all the other architectural elements in its fabric remained in the neo-Classical tradition. In respect to this anomaly, St. Mary's is like St. Paul's Cathedral in London, which, although executed in the neo-Classical Renaissance style, has the floor layout of a large medieval Gothic church.

So while much has changed at St. Mary's since 1790, much remains the same. Most of the small panes of glass in the large, round-headed nave windows are those installed more than two hundred years ago when large sheets of glass were unavailable. Only in the east window, where a fine portrait of the Blessed Virgin Mary and Child was installed in 1895, has the original glass been replaced. The old plaster on the walls still retains as part of its composition quahog shells left nearby on the Fundy shore by dispossessed Acadian settlers as they awaited transport into exile in 1755. And most of the original shingles remain on the walls, fastened to wide, old, hand-hewn boards with the square-headed, Nova-Scotia-forged nails that were brought by soldiers on their backs ninety miles from Halifax, on foot, in the spring of 1790. The finish of the church — from the decorative wooden keystones in the window surrounds and the pediments that adorn the exterior gables, to the cornices and fluted columns of the interior — is superb.

The architect and builder of St. Mary's Church was William Matthews, from the military ordnance department in Halifax. Much of it is of pine, felled and milled locally. The soil in Auburn is sandy, and hospitable to pine — although today there are few specimens left as magnificent as the trees that ended up in the fabric of St. Mary's Church.

Its first rector was the Reverend John Wiswall, a Loyalist and former Congregationalist minister who had taken Anglican orders in 1764 and seen his church at Portland, Maine, burned by rebels in 1775. Its first benefactor was Colonel James Morden (after whom the nearby village of Morden, on the Bay of Fundy, is named), who played a role similar to that performed by the lord of the manor in an English country parish. A chalice and paten given by Bishop Inglis in 1790, a 1753 Bible, two long-handled wooden collection boxes, panels bearing the coats of arms of King George III and of the diocese of Nova Scotia — both said to have been painted by Bishop Inglis himself to hang over the governor's and the bishop's pews respectively — and two panels bearing the Ten Commandments and the Lord's Prayer flanking the holy table on the east wall are among the treasures preserved in St. Mary's Church.

Of course, the church itself is its own chief treasure. But wooden churches are vulnerable to fire, and two-hundred-year-old timbers particularly so. St. Mary's has had at least one very close call with fire. On the night of Saturday, September 20, 1981, at 2:45 a.m., the spire of the church was hit by lightning and set ablaze. A crowd gathered, and four fire departments from nearby towns arrived only to discover that their ladders and the pressure in their hoses were inadequate to get water to where the flames were burning down the length of the spire. The rector, the Reverend Langley MacLean, called on all present to pray that the church might be saved. Some knelt and some stood — and the prayer was answered almost immediately: a gust of wind carried the water to the flames, and the fire was put out. Father MacLean claimed credit not only for the prayer, but also for his having sprinkled the entire building with holy water two weeks earlier!

When St. Mary's was built in 1790, documents relating to its construction were placed in a gilded copper ball on the weathervane on the spire. Several times over the years the ball has fallen to the ground, usually in windstorms, and each time the documents have been copied and replaced in the ball on its return to the spire. In 1981, the old documents suffered water damage and had to be dried out and sent to Ottawa for restoration. This time copies were placed in the ball when it was put back. A lightning arrestor was added, made in the shape of a cross.

In 1986, the 1891 vestry on the north side of the chancel was replaced by a small church-hall building, designed by architect Ron Peck to blend architecturally with the church.

St. Mary's is the earliest of seven Charles-Inglis-era churches in the Annapolis Valley. The others are at Clementsport (St. Edward's, built in 1795), Karsdale (St. Paul's/Christ Church, 1791–1794), Granville Centre (1814–1826), and Annapolis Royal (St. Luke's, 1815–1822) at the western end of the Valley, Cornwallis (St. John's, 1804–1810) near the eastern end, and old Holy Trinity at Middleton (1789–1791) in the middle, twelve miles west of Auburn. The Cornwallis and Granville Centre churches are so similar to St. Mary's in their proportions and fenestration as to suggest that they, too, were drawn by William Matthews. Holy Trinity, Middleton, and St. Edward's, Clementsport, have been replaced for regular use by Gothic Revival alternatives built a century later. In Middleton, the town grew up a mile or so east of the church, making its location inconvenient to a majority of the parishioners. At Clementsport, the location of St. Edward's at the top of a hill prompted the erection of

a new building lower down in order to spare worshippers the steep climb — although the factor that determined the decision to construct the new church might well have been less the steep climb and more the erection of a Baptist church at the foot of the hill. In both cases, the old churches became neglected and dilapidated through disuse, only to be rescued and restored as the twentieth century advanced

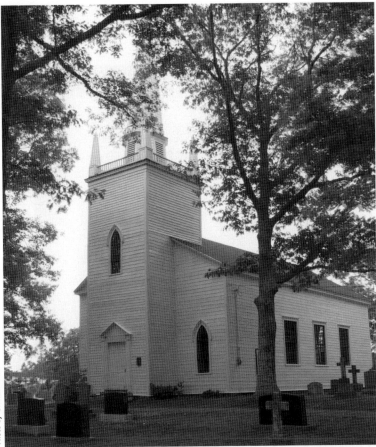

Photo by Graham Tuck.

Photo by Graham Tuck.

More Inglis-era churches, previous page top and bottom: St. Edward's, Clementsport, 1795; All Saints', Granville Centre, 1791–1826; top left: Holy Trinity, Middleton, 1789–91; above: St. John's, Cornwallis, 1804–12.

and brought with it a growing appreciation of heritage architecture. Because these buildings are not used very often, they have undergone little change. Stepping into St. Edward's, with its box pews, white plastered walls, small-paned and round-headed windows, and old pine woodwork is like going back in time into the eighteenth century.

One might think that the concentration of these Colonial-era Anglican churches in the Annapolis Valley indi-

cates a large and flourishing Anglican population in that part of Nova Scotia at the end of the eighteenth century. In actual fact, they were built, with the assistance in many cases of government money, to try to stem the tide of enthusiasm that had swept in from New England before the American rebellion and that many Loyalists — particularly Charles Inglis — perceived as being subversive not only of decency and order, but also of attachment to the Crown.

St. George's, Sydney, 1785–91, was built with stone taken from the dismantled French fortress of Louisberg.

Photo by Graham Tuck.

Chapter Four
Barrington, Grand Pré, and North West: Meet for the Sabbath

IN 1758 THE GOVERNOR OF Nova Scotia, Charles Lawrence, invited people in New England to come to Nova Scotia and settle the rich agricultural lands in the Annapolis Valley, the Minas Basin, and the Chignecto isthmus, lying vacant by reason of his recent expulsion of the Acadians, whose home they had been for more than a hundred years. No fewer than eight thousand New Englanders, chiefly from Massachusetts, Connecticut, and Rhode Island, took up his offer in the 1760s. Many fishermen came as well, especially from Massachusetts, long accustomed to fishing in Nova Scotia waters and attracted by promises of land with no payments due for ten years. They settled around the southwestern shore, the part of Nova Scotia most easily reached from places like Gloucester and Boston.

These New England planters, as they were called (an old English name for settlers), were largely descendants of English dissenters, or nonconformists, who had immigrated to the New World rather than conform to the doctrine and discipline of the established Church of England. In New England, most of them had been brought up in Congregationalist churches, which, as the name implies, were self-governing; but in Nova Scotia, several of the ministers who served the Congregationalist congregations returned to New England to support the rebellion against England that broke out in 1775. Many Congregationalists in Nova Scotia then became swept up in the revivalist New Light movement, as it was called, preached by charismatic men like William Black and Henry Alline, which also had its roots in New England, where it was called The Great Awakening. The spiritual lineage of many of Nova Scotia's Baptists today leads back through the New Light to the Congregationalism of the New England planters. Indeed, Baptist churches in their polity are substantially autonomous and self-governing, very much as were the old Congregationalists, or Independents (as they were called in England).

So it was that forty families came from Cape Cod to take up 100,000 acres at Barrington in 1761.

The first few years were occupied in hewing habitations for humans out of the forest, and it wasn't until 1765 that work began on a house of God. Joshua Nickerson, a local

Photo by Graham Tuck.

The Meeting House, Barrington, 1765: exterior.

shipbuilder and millwright, was in charge of the project, assisted by carpenter Elijah Swaine, a Quaker from Nantucket. The meeting house they built is still standing, thirty-six feet long and thirty feet wide. Its entrance is in one long wall and its principal piece of furniture, the pulpit, stands against the centre of the wall opposite. A gallery runs along overhead inside the entrance and end elevations. When the first exercises (as the services were called) were held in 1767, there were still no windows, seats, or stoves in the building. At that time it had two doors, one in each end, and was more than a little barn-like. But it was neatly finished on the outside and clapboarded. Today the clapboards are gone, replaced by shingles.

During exercises, men and women were segregated, and children sat on a long, log timber in front of the pulpit, facing the congregation. Henry Alline preached in the meeting

Photo by Graham Tuck.

The Meeting House, Barrington: view from the gallery.

Photo by Graham Tuck.

The Meeting House, Barrington: view from the ground floor.

house in 1780, and in 1786, so did the Wesleyan preacher, Freeborn Garrettson, who described the building as still being "without doors, windows or pews."[11]

The first minister was the Reverend Samuel Wood, from Connecticut, who remained four years. The settlers lacked the money with which to pay him a stipend, so he was given instead a grant of land at Wood's Harbour.

As time passed, the Congregationalist identity of the building faded, and in 1814 a board of trustees declared it open to "all preachers of the gospel." It wasn't until 1841 that

Photo by R.C. Tuck.

The Covenanters' Church, Grand Pré, 1804. The steeple was added in 1818.

the building was plastered inside, fitted with box pews, and furnished with a stove and chimney. Leadership in these improvements was provided by the Presbyterians and, for a time, the meeting house was known as The Kirk and as Saint John's Church. Later in the nineteenth century it was used by Baptists, and in 1889 the trustees of the meeting house were given permission by an act of the provincial legislature to raze the building, which at that time had become quite dilapidated. However, the demolition was postponed when the clerk of the trustees became ill. By the time he had recovered, friends of the meeting house had rallied to its defence and the building was saved. From 1917 until the early 1930s it was used by the local Anglican congregation. In 1933 the care of the building passed into the hands of the Cape Sable Historical Society, which continues to look after it on behalf of the Nova Scotia Museum and the province of Nova Scotia — owners of the meeting house since 1979.

At Grand Pré, the Covenanters' Church is similar in concept and layout to that of the Barrington Meeting House. The

Photo by Graham Tuck.

The Covenanters' Church, Grand Pré: interior.

entrance doorway is set in the centre of one long side of a rectangular building with a triple-decker pulpit on the opposite wall. Box pews are set against the walls, with a centre section of pews below the pulpit divided in two by an alley that runs straight from the door to the pulpit. A gallery runs around three sides of the interior, as at Barrington, and is accessed by stairs in the tower, which also serves as a vestry. The Covenanter's Church is set on a hill and was built 1804–11.

on that last awful day in 1755 before they were bundled into British ships and sailed away into exile. It is not a church, however, but a museum. One enters it expecting to find an altar, statues of saints, and a prie-dieu at which to kneel and bewail the sorrow that befell the folk who cleared and diked and settled and farmed these Minas meadows; but no, there are instead glass cases containing fragments of their lives dug out of the ground by archaeologists.

Below the hill in the meadows that border the Minas Basin is a modern replica of the church in which the earlier Acadian inhabitants worshipped, and in which they were assembled

The meeting house at North West (i.e. northwest of Lunenburg) near Mahone Bay dates from 1820, but its origins are earlier than that, in missions preached in the 1790s by an

Photo by Graham Tuck.

The Meeting House, North West, 1820.

itinerant evangelist from near Windsor, in the Annapolis Valley, named Joseph Dimock. According to his account, his appearance in the community was not universally welcomed, and on one occasion a mob turned up and attempted to deter him from preaching by pelting him with snowballs.[12] Nevertheless, a church was organized with ten members in 1809, and the decision to erect the meeting house followed in 1818. It is the property today of the United Baptist Church.

Unlike the meeting houses at Barrington and Grand Pré, the entrance to the North West church is set in a gabled end elevation (although the building is almost square in the proportions of its footprint), a little off-centre. The pulpit is a reading desk placed on the front of a wide platform on the far wall opposite the doorway that also accommodates the choir; this arrangement, and the three-light Gothic window in the wall behind appear to be later in date than the building itself, and replace an original high pulpit. A narthex runs the width of the building inside the entrance, with stairways to the gallery at one end and to the basement, excavated by volunteers in the 1970s, at the other. The exterior is clapboarded with corner board pilasters characteristic of the Regency period, and together with the proportions of the building betray its age, despite the otherwise nearly new appearance of its wooden, freshly painted fabric.

Chapter Five
The Round Church of St. George, Halifax:
Coming up Roses

AFTER THE BRITISH GOVERNMENT RETURNED Louisburg to France in 1748 (it had been captured by New Englanders three years before), it decided it must develop its presence in mainland Nova Scotia, which it had held since 1714, as a counterweight to the French fortress. Halifax was founded in 1749, but many of the city dwellers brought out from England to populate it were unable to cope with the severe winters, primitive conditions, and disease; some died, and others left. A hardier type of settler was needed, and London found them in the foreign Protestants it recruited in Germany, the Montbeliard region of France, and Switzerland. They were brought to Halifax, where many from an urban background with marketable skills quickly found a niche; others, in number about fifteen hundred, more experienced in agriculture and rural pursuits, were moved in 1753 to Mirligaiche on the South Shore, which they renamed Lunenburg.

The foreign Protestants from Germany were Lutheran and those from Switzerland and Montbeliard Calvinist or Reformed; but the English established church was Anglican. Because Nova Scotia was an English colony, inevitably there was an anticipation on the part of the governing authorities that the foreign Protestants would eventually become Anglican. Not all of them did, by any means; but so many did that by the middle of the twentieth century Lunenburg County, with the lowest percentage of Anglo-Saxon surnames of any county in Nova Scotia, was said to have a higher percentage of Anglicans in its population than any other.

In Halifax, in 1756, a small house was acquired and moved "by the united effort of voluntary hands"[13] to a new site on Brunswick Street in the north end and made into "the German church of St. George."[14] Although the Germans worshipped and governed themselves according to their own evangelical Lutheran tradition, the church technically was a chapel-of-ease of St. Paul's, whose clergy came twice a year to administer Holy Communion. When the building was enlarged in 1761, with financial assistance from the government, and given a small steeple (in which was hung a bell purloined from the French at the fall of Louisburg), it was blessed by the rector of St. Paul's, the Reverend John Breynton, in both English and German. It is still standing,

Photo by H.M. Scott Smith.

St. George's Church, Halifax, 1800: view from Brunswick Street.

essentially unchanged, and continues to be known today, as it was in the eighteenth century, as the "Little Dutch Church" — a misreading of "*Deutch*," which was, of course, the Germans' name for themselves.

In 1894, road works on Brunswick Street made necessary the reconstruction of the foundation of the Little Dutch Church, in the course of which burial vaults, and a burial pit containing remains of persons believed to have perished in

Photo by Graham Tuck.

St. George's Church, Halifax: interior set up for a recital.

(1715–85), his wife Anna (1724–84) — early leaders in the German congregation — and the Reverend Bernard Houseal (1727–99), a Loyalist Lutheran clergyman who, like Charles Inglis, fled New York on American independence, and after ordination in England as an Anglican priest in 1785, became rector of St. George's in 1786.

By 1799 there were English as well as Germans in St. George's congregation, and a process of assimilation of the Germans into the English-speaking community was underway. When, after Houseal's death, the churchwardens petitioned the governor for another German minister, the English element in the congregation apparently objected, and the Reverend George Wright, an Irishman who was curate of St. Paul's, was appointed instead. He reported to the Society for the Propagation of the Gospel, "The congregation were originally all Germans; but now so intermixed and intermarried with the other inhabitants, and so much used to English manners and language that very few of them retain their own, at least they all speak English much better than they do German." He described them as "industrious, abstemious, honest and persevering, and very loyal subjects."[15]

By this time, the Little Dutch Church was much too small for the growing north end Halifax population. A new church was needed, and in 1800 it was built — a round drum in the Palladian style, topped by a cupola that sat on a dome. The round floor plan has long been attributed to Edward, Duke of Kent, son of King George III, father of Queen Victoria, commander of the garrison at Halifax from 1794 until August 1800, an amateur architect whose love of round buildings is also reflected in the still-standing band house he built at Prince's Lodge on Bedford Basin.

a typhus epidemic in 1750, were found under the church. In the early 1990s these burials were again examined, this time scientifically, when the floor of the church was taken up and rebuilt, lest it prove inadequate to support the weight of German Chancellor Helmut Kohl, a heavy man, and others scheduled to visit Halifax for the G7 summit in 1995. The individuals in the vaults were identified as Otto Schwartz

The Little Dutch Church, Halifax, 1756.

In 1822, the new St. George's was enlarged by the addition of a chancel that accommodated an altar and choir stalls, and an entry porch that sheltered a narthex and the wide flight of stairs required to access the building from Brunswick Street. Were these additions part of the original concept for the building? In 1802 a debt of more than £900 remained on St. George's, a possible reason for leaving the building incomplete. Five years later, the Society for the Propagation of the Gospel was asked to assist in the completion of the church, which it agreed to do provided that "no other Divine Service be performed therein but that of the Established Church of England."[16] On May 31, 1808, the elders and churchwardens presented a declaration to Bishop Charles Inglis asserting that St. George's "is and at all times hereafter shall be held by them and their successors as a Church of the Established Religion."[17] But they went on to say that they intended to retain their original form of church government, which required that occupancy of the offices of elder and church-warden be restricted to Germans and their descendants. This was not acceptable to the bishop. In 1811, the Governor, Sir George Prevost, caused £500 to be set aside for St. George's, but whether or not St. George's would actually get the money was to depend upon the bishop's approval of the grant. The elders and wardens replied by saying that they would agree to adopt the Anglican form of parish government by rector, wardens, and vestry, but that the Germans in the congregation should have a veto over any non-German elected to office. This also was not acceptable to Bishop Inglis, and he told them that he could neither "take any steps towards the appropriation of those sums as you desire" nor consecrate the building in its unfinished condition.[18] The German congregation replied in May, 1812, that "as they have as much money as will repair the Chapel from leaking they will compleat that part as soon as the season will permit it."[19] In 1818, the Reverend Benjamin Gerrish Gray succeeded George Wright as minister at St. George's, and the Society for the Propagation of the Gospel informed the church that it would not contribute to his stipend as it had to his predecessors' until German privilege was eliminated and the regular Anglican system of parochial government adopted.

This did the trick, and in 1819 the bishop (by this time Stanser) was "humbly requested to certify to His Excellency the Governor that the Congregation are entitled to receive the Donation of His Excellency the late Sir George Prevost

and to request that the five hundred pounds now lying in the Provincial Treasury be applied to the use of this Church." Three years later, the chancel and the entry porch were built and St. George's was substantially complete.

As the years passed, St. George's became less and less identified with the Germans, who became more and more assimilated into the general population. During the lengthy incumbency of the Reverend Robert Uniacke, 1825–1870, it became, in Brian Cuthbertson's striking phrase, a place of "evangelical fervour and good works." Those members of St. Paul's upset in the Great Disruption of 1825 who did not become Baptists became members of St. George's congregation. The galleries that ringed the interior of the building in ascending circles were occupied by soldiers and sailors from the citadel and the dockyard, Sunday school children, and the servants of the gentry who sat down below in the body of the church in box pews.

As Halifax grew, St. George's, with St. Paul's, spawned daughter churches — St. John's, St. James's, St. Matthias's, and St. Mark's. Trinity Church grew out of the old Garrison Chapel that stood between St. George's and St. Paul's. But after the Second World War, dingy housing in whole areas of the city served by several of these churches, much of it thrown up after the Halifax explosion in 1917, was demolished and replaced with shopping centres and office buildings. Canon Gary Thorne, rector of St. George's in 2000, described the consequences:

> By the mid-seventies the programme of urban renewal had taken its toll. Even with the construction of several large seniors' high

rises, and the influx of many African Nova Scotians (dislodged by the demolition of Africville, their village on the shore of Bedford Basin) into public housing in Uniacke Square and Mulgrave Park, the population of the North End was reduced by a whopping 42 percent between 1961 and 1976. Social stigma attached to public housing kept people with money away from the north end ... all of the bank branches, as well as the local supermarket, closed ... even telephone booths were removed from the area because of repeated vandalism.

It became the neighbourhood of the homeless, "persons who at one time or another might have found a welcome place in a nursing home or a mental institution, or who find themselves homeless because of borderline personality traits or lifestyles, or because of a combination of lost jobs, marriage breakdowns, welfare benefit cuts, chronic depression, drug addictions, wrong choices, lack of personal support..." St. George's worshipping congregation began more and more to be made up of people who had moved from the old neighbourhood to elsewhere in the city, but whose family ties with the church kept them coming, at least for a time. Early in the post-war period St. George's became a home away from home for Newfoundlanders living in Halifax, attracted by clergy who, like themselves, had their roots in The Rock. In the 1980s, it became the Prayer Book Catholic parish in Halifax, the refuge of Anglicans unable to accommodate themselves to the Book of Alternative Services, the Anglican version of the Vatican II Roman Catholic vernacular liturgy, the widespread implementation of which made many Anglicans feel homeless in their own churches.

Then one day in June 1994, several small boys from the neighbourhood broke into St. George's through a cellar hatch that had once served to admit deliveries of coal, and found their way to the choir room. Having some matches with them, they set fire to the choir robes hanging around the room to see if they would burn. Within a few hours, 40

Photo by Jim MacSwain, courtesy of *The Anglican Free Press*

The Reverend Garry Thorne and two parishioners watch St. George's burn.

percent of St. George's Church had been destroyed, chiefly the dome with its cupola, and the entry built in 1822. It would cost millions of dollars to rebuild it.

But would it be rebuilt? At least one of the nearby churches, subject to the same challenges of depopulation and social change as St. George's, was said to covet its congregation. And not a few diocesan officials felt that the Anglican Church had far too many churches downtown and saw the fire as an opportunity to be rid of at least one of them. Others resented what they saw as the backwardness and stuffiness of St. George's in its rejection of Alternative Services and what has been called the "Happy Clappy style" of worship that was catching on in some places, and its desire to continue to use the Book of Common Prayer. The congregation was given six months to prepare a proposal for the future of St. George's to present to the Bishop of Nova Scotia, the Right Reverend Arthur Peters.

But was St. George's just another church? Was it dispensable? Wouldn't Halifax — indeed, Nova Scotia and Canada itself — be poorer without St. George's, quite apart from its tradition of worship and its soup kitchen and all the other ministries that went on in it and from it, and for which it mattered to a number of local people? The building itself was unique, a treasure of heritage architecture that surely ought not to be lost if it were at all possible to save it. Its congregation rallied to its defence, and enlisted so much support from government in the community and across the country that it became impossible for the bishop to refuse permission for it to be rebuilt, even if he had wanted to. But in giving the restoration his blessing, he cautioned that St. George's must be a "responsible parish whose primary ministry is to people."

However, Dr. Margaret Casey, director of the North End Health Clinic for twenty years (and a non-Anglican), put the case for restoring St. George's better than anyone else when, as Canon Thorne reported, "she encouraged us to do everything we could to restore the Round Church because of the necessity for roses as well as bread in all our lives."

Then, just as the rebuilding of St. George's was in its final stages, late on Halloween night 2001, St. John's Church in Lunenburg, built by the German and Swiss Foreign Protestants in 1754, the year after they left Halifax, was set on fire, apparently by Halloween hooligans (although that has never been proven), and much of it — like St. George's — was destroyed. But this time, in Lunenburg, there was no hesitation as to what to do, for what had been learned, and achieved, at St. George's provided Lunenburg with a precedent and pattern to follow. St. John's parishioners voted by a margin of 91 percent to restore their church as it had been before. And the architect who had successfully supervised the restoration of St. George's, Ron Calhoun, was hired to do the same job at St. John's.

Chapter Six
Saint John's, Lunenburg:
South Shore Phoenix

THE ST. JOHN'S CHURCH, LUNENBURG, which burned on Halloween 2001, was, architecturally, largely the work of David Stirling, a Halifax architect who had been trained in his native Scotland and engaged by the Lunenburg Anglican parish in 1870 to Gothicize their old Georgian-style building that dated back to 1754. It had been erected in that year in the principal square of the newly laid out town at the expense (£476) of the Lords of Trade & Plantation, using timbers brought from Boston.

The settlers, mostly Germans from the Palatinate in Western Germany with a smaller number of French-speaking people from Montbeliard and Switzerland, in all about fifteen hundred persons, were accompanied by the Reverend Jean-Baptiste Moreau, his wife, Elizabeth de la Bertauche, and their four-year-old son, Cornwallis, said to be the first baby born in Halifax. Moreau was a former prior of the St-Mathieu monastery in Brittany who had left France and been received into the Church of England. He had been sent to Nova Scotia in 1749 by The Society for the Propagation of the Gospel to try to persuade the Acadians, who had been under British rule since 1715, to convert to the Church of England, but he had been unsuccessful (in 1755 the British expelled the Acadians from the colony), and was now happy to be on his way to Lunenburg as chaplain to the French-speaking Foreign Protestants. The British authorities also tried to find a minister fluent in German to minister to the Lutherans, but it was not until 1767 that the Reverend Paulus Bryzelius, a German-speaking Swede who had ministered to Lutherans and Moravians in Pennsylvania, was ordained priest at the age of fifty-four by the bishop of London and sent to Lunenburg as rector of St. John's Church. Until then, the settlement's majority (German inhabitants) had to listen to Moreau's sermons in English or French, which are said to have averaged an hour and a half in length; and only the year before, the Lutherans and the Calvinists in Lunenburg had assembled materials with which to build a church they planned to share between them.

The newly arrived settlers had made Sunday worship a priority right from their first week in Lunenburg. Colonel Charles Lawrence, who was in charge of the new settlement, wrote to the governor:

St. John's Church, Lunenburg, 1754: the round tower was replaced in 1840.

I am desired by the body of the people to move your Excellency for board and nails for putting up some kind of fabric wherein they may have Divine Service. The labour they (being devoutly disposed) say they will cheerfully give. In this I must own I'd wish they were indulged: for altho' they are unrighteous enough in other respects yet in their public worship they seem serious and decent.

The money provided by the Lords of Trade and Plantation proved to be insufficient to finish the building. It was not until nine years later, in 1763, that a grant of £259 from The Society for the Propagation of the Gospel enabled the settlers to finish it by adding windows and a gallery — and thirty-three thousand shingles to the leaking roof. Like many of the churches (of all denominations) erected in Nova Scotia in the eighteenth century, it was designed with a gallery running around three sides of the interior, with square-headed windows in the lower range under the gallery, and (probably) round-headed ones in the upper range in its side elevations. As was common in many Anglican churches of the period, a centrally placed triple-decker pulpit dominated the interior, obscuring the small altar table placed behind it, inside the rail at which the communicants knelt to receive the infrequently celebrated Sacrament. Some time later, a round tower with a conical cap in the Teutonic style was added. The church was sixty feet long and forty feet wide, and for many years had no pews or heating system.

At first, St. John's Church was used by all the traditions represented in the settlement's population, Lutheran and Reformed, as well as Anglican. When Bryzelius proved to be a great success as a preacher in both German and English, it looked as if the Lutheran and Reformed plan to erect a second church in the town might come to naught, for a local magistrate reported to the lieutenant-governor that Bryzelius moved people to tears as they listened to him preaching to them in their own tongue. He said the gallery was so crowded with men that there were fears its railing would collapse and spill its occupants into the ground floor, which by custom was where the women sat, flanked by the elders of the congregation.

Sebastien Zouberbuhler, a native of Switzerland, perhaps the only resident of Lunenburg proficient in all three languages — French, German, and English — and a member of the legislative assembly and council, wanted Lunenburg to remain a community of only one church. Ironically, it was Bryzelius himself who unintentionally precipitated the breakdown of the Lunenburg population into religious denominations. Before he left England, Bryzelius had been given a prayer book in German by the Reverend F.M. Ziegenhagen, chaplain to King George II, which he used in celebrating the Holy Communion in Lunenburg. However, when he discovered that the Germans in Halifax were using a Book of Common Prayer in German "printed by authority" he decided he ought to use it instead, and asked The Society for the Propagation of the Gospel to send three hundred copies of it to Lunenburg.[20] His congregation noticed the difference between the two books, however, and suspected him of trying to force them into conformity to the Church of England. The Lutherans and Calvinists then withdrew from St. John's and built their own churches. On Good Friday, 1773, Bryzelius suffered a stroke while in the pulpit, and was buried directly beneath it, leaving a widow and nine children "in distressed circumstances." He and Moreau and fifteen others are buried underneath St. John's Church.

The loss of the Lutherans and the Calvinists (i.e. the Reformed or Presbyterians) created difficulty for St. John's, which became the smallest of three congregations. When the Reverend Peter de la Roche arrived as rector of St. John's in 1771, he reported that St. John's congregation consisted mostly of Germans who understood English. By 1795, the Lutheran church numbered 175 families, the Calvinists 143 and the Anglicans about 70.

However, by the middle of the nineteenth century St. John's had rebounded. Basil Brownless, the St. John's parish historian, credits "an elite group of families headed by the Creighton, Rudolf, Kaulbach and Zwicker families ... Tories ... who dominated the political, social and economic life of the town" and made St. John's "a fashionable place to attend." This was the congregation consisting "mostly of Germans who understood English." Its members had prospered, but the large Lutheran congregation, which continued to worship in German, had become something of an ethnic ghetto. Jealousy of the Anglican Church emerged in Lunenburg, and focussed on St. John's having ownership of the central square in the town, which had been deeded to it by the lieutenant-governor in 1820. All the other squares in the town were publicly owned. In the 1850s, Liberal members attempted several times to put a bill through the Nova Scotia Legislative Assembly that would take control of the square away from St. John's Church; but the bill was dropped in 1858 when St. John's promised never to sell, lease, or build upon that part of the square not occupied by the church building. Thus the square was preserved as a public space, and at no expense to the public for its upkeep!

As the nineteenth century got into its second half, its churches prospered and denominational rivalry flourished in Lunenburg. They began to enlarge their buildings. By this time the Methodists had also arrived on the scene, and their church building in the end turned out to be bigger than any of the others. St. John's, as the oldest, was smaller and old-fashioned, and it also had the most conservative membership. But that was soon to change.

The first change in the building was modest enough. By 1840 its round tower had become dilapidated and had to be replaced. A new tower was built from the ground up, twelve feet square and seventy feet high, with Gothic-style pinnacles at its four corners, designed by William Lawson, a local schoolmaster. It incorporated an entrance porch, stairways to the gallery, a vestry, a bellringer's chamber, and a "singing pew." Otherwise, though, the church remained as it had been for nearly a hundred years — a galleried Georgian

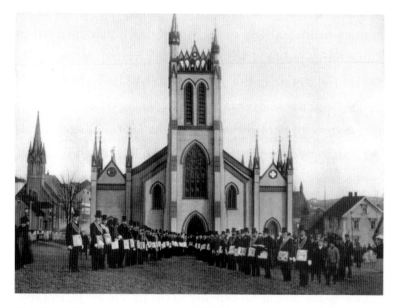

St. John's Church, Lunenburg, c.1900. Its restoration after the fire of 2001 was designed to be faithful to its appearance 1892–1915, following the "Great Reconstructions" of 1872 and 1892. This photograph was made on the occasion of a Church parade by members of the Masonic Lodge, a formidable body of men in Lunenburg County one hundred years ago. St. Andrew's Presbyterian Church is shown on the left.

preaching box, its interior dominated by a centrally placed three-decker pulpit.

It was the sort of church that Hibbert Binney, who had succeeded John Inglis as bishop of Nova Scotia in 1851, disliked intensely. But his first communication with the parish was to rebuke it for its failure to pay its rector: "I am sorry to find that the payments promised to your rector are a year and a half in arrears," he wrote. "I must accordingly remove him to some other place, and of course I cannot send any other minister to Lunenburg to starve." The parishioners grumbled that the parish was in debt because it had bought a rectory and built the tower, but they promised to meet their obligations to their rector in the future. So Binney sent them the Reverend Dr. Henry Owen, like himself a graduate of Oxford University, and sympathetic to the Oxford Movement that sought to renew Catholic devotion in the English church.

It took Owen close to twenty years to effect the changes he wanted in St. John's Church. It wasn't until after a Church Improvement Committee was formed in 1867 — and an episcopal visit from Binney in which he rebuked the parishioners for having a church that was too small and had no chancel, a flat ceiling, a pulpit in front of the altar, and boards under the seats that made kneeling difficult — that St. John's began to bestir itself. In April of 1870, the congregation met and endorsed what became known as The Great Reconstruction.

The architect chosen to rebuild St. John's was David Stirling, a native of Galashiels in Scotland, who had spent time in St. John's, Newfoundland, before settling in Halifax. He was a master of the early Gothic Revival, capable of producing correct designs in either the Early English or Geometric style.

He moved the building twenty-five feet to the west to make room at the other end for a new apsidal chancel and sanctuary, and, with ten feet added to its length, the old church became the nave of the new one. The galleries and flat ceiling were demolished, a splendid hammerbeam roof was built, and tall, single-light, early English Gothic style windows with hood-moulds (a Stirling signature) were cut in the walls. At the same time the 1840 tower was dressed up, with new pinnacles at the corners connected by arcades of small arches, and in its western elevation a large window with Geometric tracery was opened below the double lancets of the bell chamber.

The reconstruction was complete in 1872, and Binney came and rededicated the building, this time with only words of praise for the parishioners.

The years that followed were a prosperous time in Lunenburg. A large, new Methodist Church was built in 1885, and a new Lutheran Church, capable of accommodating four hundred and fifty in its nave and an additional hundred in an annex, was built in 1888. In the same year, St. John's congregation decided that it too must be bigger — although it had been enlarged less than twenty years before. This time the congregation voted not to engage an architect, and the project was entrusted to master carpenter Solomon Morash and a team of carpenters, and completed in 1892.

He enlarged the church by the addition of side aisles to the nave. The walls, with their lancet windows, were simply moved outwards on each side and replaced by piers encased in octagonal sheaths and given a marbleized finish. On the exterior, corner posts and buttresses were topped by fourteen slender, four-sided pinnacles, with gabled bases accommodating trefoil decoration. The exuberance of these pin-

nacles became muted when they were replaced in 1915 by shingled spikes, no doubt because they had proven vulnerable to the moist climate of the Atlantic coast. In 1936, the church was painted white with black trim, an inappropriate choice for a High Victorian Gothic Revival style building, which always looks best in colour.

Much of this fabric was destroyed in the fire in 2001 and had to be refashioned in the restoration of 2003. But most of the furniture, including a richly carved altar made in 1926, remained undamaged or repairable, and many of the stained glass windows and memorial plaques survived the fire, although with various degrees of injury. A grievous loss was the mechanism of the carillon in the tower. Its ten bells, the largest weighing eighteen hundred pounds, survived, although three were damaged and were recast at the same bell foundry in Ohio they had come from in 1902. Several of the windows were badly broken and had to be painstakingly reassembled from pieces collected from where they had fallen on the ground. A massive plastic cocoon was erected around the ruins and the 50 percent of the building lost in the fire rebuilt inside it. The restoration was so faithful that the fourteen pinnacles were reconstructed to their original 1892 design.

One might ask, "Is the rebuilt St. John's the old St. John's? And was the St. John's of 1872 or 1892 the St. John's of 1754?"

Well, yes and no. Perhaps St. John's is less its fabric at any one point in time and more its identity across time. Perhaps it is like the seventeen people whose mortal remains are interred under the church, the most recent as long ago as 1826. Those persons no longer have much or any material existence where they are, down there in the ground, but they continue to be real as identities. Perhaps that is why the people of St. John's in 2001 voted 91 percent to restore their church, rather than

Photo by Edward A. Jordan

replace it or create a replica of it. Their own identity mattered to them, and so did St. John's. That is why its loss was such a blow. Now, in the resurrection of St. John's, there is also the suggestion of a greater resurrection. The parishioners were not prepared to accept the idea that an evil, or death itself — i.e. an act of arson, or the fire — should have the last word, either in respect to their church, or themselves.

The ruins of St. John's Church, Lunenburg, being encased in the plastic "bubble" in the early winter of 2001–2, inside which the exterior of the church was restored.

Chapter Seven
St. Mary's Basilica, Halifax:
Seeing God's Word

IN 1782, THIRTY-THREE YEARS after the founding of Halifax, the repeal of laws that prohibited Roman Catholics from holding public office, and their church from owning land and building houses of worship, enabled the purchase by some Irish Catholics of a property in Halifax on the corner of Barrington Street and Spring Garden Road, and the erection on it in 1784 of a small church dedicated to St. Peter. The congregation of St. Peter's grew with the city, and after Halifax was made a missionary diocese separate from Quebec in 1817, its bishop — who, first as the Reverend Edmund Burke, and then as vicar apostolic of Nova Scotia and titular bishop of Sion, had been serving St. Peter's since 1801 — set out in 1820 to replace St. Peter's with a cathedral built of stone.

The new church was also given a new dedication — to Saint Mary. It was 104 feet long and built of the local ironstone with a sandstone front elevation on Spring Garden Road. There were, on each side of its nave, two ranges of eight windows, one above and one below, the heads in the upper range pointed with intersecting tracery and those in the lower range square-headed. Inside the church, a gallery ran around three sides of the building, as in St. Paul's, a couple of blocks along Barrington Street to the north. The proportions of the building, its interior finish, and the slope of its roof (the original hand-hewn timbers of 1820 are still in place) were thoroughly Georgian, despite the pointed windows. It was the second Roman Catholic cathedral to be built in what is today Canada.

But by 1860 the Gothic Revival in architecture was well underway, and St. Mary's inevitably had acquired an old-fashioned look. So Archbishop Thomas Connolly engaged a New York architect, Patrick Keely, who is said to have designed four hundred churches, to Gothicize St. Mary's. He removed the galleries along the east and west walls and, by extending the building ninety-six feet to the north, not only made good the lost seating, but added to it. The removal of the gallery enabled each pair of upper and lower windows to be joined, making one window in each bay audaciously tall in relation to its width. The essence of Gothic architecture is its upward thrust, and this change in the windows, together

St. Mary's Basilica, Halifax, 1820: view from Barrington Street.

Photo by Graham Tuck.

Photo by Graham Tuck.

St. Mary's Basilica, Halifax: the nave, looking to the high altar.

with the replacement of the neo-Classical columns that had supported the gallery by twin arcades of narrow piers with clustered shafts soaring from the floor to the new rib-vaulted ceiling high above brilliantly transformed a rather pedestrian Georgian building into a Gothic marvel.

In the next decade, the front elevation on Spring Garden Road was rebuilt in granite. Out of it rose a splendid 189-foot granite spire, made complete on September 7, 1874, when a cross was placed at its top. For a hundred years this steeple adorned the streetscape in the down-

Photo by R.C. Tuck.

St. Mary's Basilica, Halifax: view from Spring Garden Road. The spire disappears against the Maritime Tel & Tel tower.

out the spire of the cathedral when it was viewed from Spring Garden Road.

On December 6, 1917, the explosion of the ammunition ship *Mont Blanc* in Halifax harbour blew out St. Mary's windows. They were replaced after the war by a unique set of depictions in stained glass of the Life of Christ in the upper portion of each window with related scenes from the Old Testament and the Apocrypha below. The windows were made in the Franz Mayer workshops in Munich, Germany, and are in memory of those who died in the Halifax Explosion. There can hardly be anywhere in Christendom a more complete and unified visualization of the Bible, or a more thoughtful presentation of the inter-relatedness of the Old and the New Testaments, than in these eighteen windows in the nave of St. Mary's Basilica.

In the 1960s, the Second Vatican Council made great changes in the Roman Catholic Church. Pope John XXIII, who called the council, in a famous phrase, "threw open the windows" of the Roman Church, which had felt itself under siege from the outbreak of the Reformation in the sixteenth century through the Enlightenment in the eighteenth. No longer would its worship be in Latin, but in the world's vernaculars; it would become less triumphalist and more ecumenical; and it would find God more in His immanence and less in His transcendence than it had since the fourth century. One of the outward and visible signs of these changes was the introduction of nave altars and the virtual abandonment of the old high altars, many of which — especially those in Baroque style — were little more than ledges attached to elaborate and ornate reredoses that sought to convey the magnificence and otherworldliness of the divine glory. In many churches, the old high altars were retained, but have

town heart of Halifax until, in an act of aesthetic vandalism, the local telephone company demolished the Capitol Theatre — one of the finest in the country — and erected on its site behind St. Mary's an office tower that blanked

remained almost unused, like vestigal parts of the ecclesiastical anatomy, the mass celebrated instead on tables set in front by priests who face their congregations across them. But in St. Mary's Basilica, the old reredos and altar were totally removed. All that now remains of the old reredos is a polychrome spire that houses the tabernacle in which the Blessed Sacrament is reserved, and of the altar only the pedestals that support the new altar table installed in 1969.

Yet the element of transcendence has been retained, despite the chaste simplicity of the altar table that now stands in the chord of the apse of St. Mary's: overhead, the roof of the apse is made of stained glass, and in it the Three Persons of the Blessed Trinity, Father, Son, and Holy Ghost, attend upon the coronation of the Blessed Virgin Mary, the Queen of Heaven — and patron of St. Mary's Basilica.

Facing Page: St. Mary's Basilica nave windows: the Gospel story from the New Testament, with corresponding references from the Old Testament, as told in pictures in eighteen stained glass windows set in the walls of the nave of the Basilica, beginning at the front on the Gospel (left hand) side:

Top:

(1a) Anna and Joachim present their daughter, Mary, in the temple in Jerusalem. According to early tradition, Joachim was a priest who served terms of duty in the temple.

(1b) Ruth 1:16. Ruth pledges her loyalty to Naomi.

(2a) St. Luke 1:28. The Annunciation: The archangel Gabriel greets Mary and tells her that she is to be mother of the Son of God.

(2b) Exodus 3:2. God calls Moses to his vocation from the burning bush.

(3a) St. Luke 1:42. The visitation of the Blessed Virgin Mary to Elizabeth: "Blessed art thou among women, and blessed is the fruit of thy womb."

(3b) Judith 13:19. Judith is honoured for having slain the Assyrian general.

(4a) St. Luke 2:11. The Birth of Jesus.

(4b) Genesis 1:27. The creation of man.

(5a) St. Matthew 2:11. The Epiphany (adoration of the Christ Child by the Magi).

(5b) 1 Kings 10:6. The queen of Sheba pays homage to Solomon.

(6a) St. Matthew 2:14. The Holy Family flees King Herod into Egypt.

(6b) 1 Samuel 19:10. King Saul attempts to kill David, the future king of Israel.

Bottom:

(7a) St. Luke 2:22. Presentation of Jesus in the temple.

(7b) Presentation of Samuel by Anna in the temple.

(8a) St. Luke 2:51. The Holy Family in Nazareth.

(8b) Tobit 1:9. The model family of Israel, Tobit and Anna with their son Tobias.

(9a) St. Luke 2:47. Reunion of Mary and Joseph with Jesus, who has been debating with the doctors in the temple.

(9b) Genesis 46:29. Reunion of Joseph with his father Israel (Jacob) in Egypt.

(10a) St. Luke 8:54. Jesus raises the daughter of Jairus.

(10b) 2 Kings 4:36. Elisha raises the son of the woman of Shunem.

(11a) St. Mark 10:14. Jesus blessing the children.

(11b) Genesis 48:15. Jacob blessing Ephraim and Mannaseh, the children of Joseph.

(12a) St. Luke 7:47. Jesus forgives the penitent woman's many sins.

(12b) Genesis 33:4. Esau is reconciled with his brother, Jacob.

Photo by Graham Tuck.

Photo by Graham Tuck.

Photo by Graham Tuck.

Above:

(13a) St. Matthew 26:26–28. Institution by Jesus of the Eucharist at the Last Supper (note Judas going out).

(13b) Genesis 14:18. Melchisedek, king of Salem, brings forth gifts of bread and wine.

(14a) St. Luke 23:46. Jesus dies on the Cross.

(14b) Genesis 22:10. Abraham is ready to offer his son, Isaac, in sacrifice to God.

(15a) St. Luke 24:5. Jesus rises from the dead.

(15b) Jonah 2:11, St. Matthew 12:40. Jonah's happy issue after his three-day sojourn in the great fish presages Jesus's Resurrection.

(16a) St. John 20:28. St. Thomas confesses "My Lord and my God" as he touches the wound in Jesus's side from which flowed water and blood (St. John 19:34).

(16b) Numbers 20:11. Moses brings water from the side of the rock in the wilderness.

(17a) Acts 1:11. The Ascension of Jesus.

(17b) 2 Kings 2:11. Elijah is taken up into Heaven.

(18a) Acts 2:4. The Holy Spirit is poured out on the Disciples of Jesus at Pentecost.

(18b) God gives Moses the Ten Commandments of the Law on Mt. Sinai.

St. Mary's Basilica Sanctuary windows:

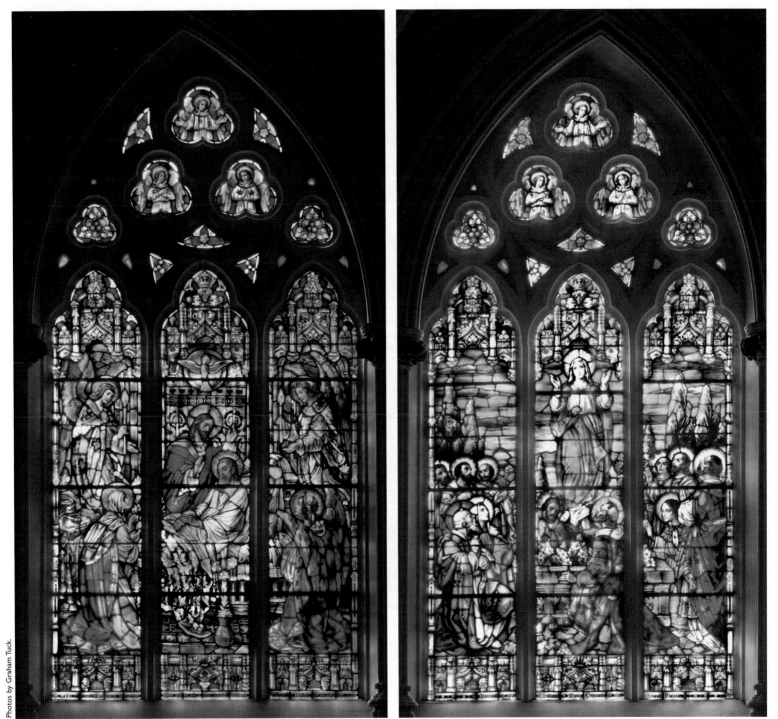

Death of St. Joseph.

Assumption of the Blessed Virgin Mary.

Photos by Graham Tuck.

Photo by Graham Tuck.

Coronation of the Blessed Virgin Mary in Heaven with the Blessed Trinity, God the Father, God the Son, and God the Holy Spirit, in attendance.

Chapter Eight
The Stirling Churches:
Neo-Gothic Debutantes

WHEN DAVID STIRLING, A NATIVE of Galashiels (near Edinburgh, in Scotland), settled in Halifax, he formed a partnership with another Scot, a businessman named Dewar who served as his office manager. Their office produced designs for courthouses, banks, and commercial buildings in neo-Romanesque or Italianate style, and plans for churches in the Early English or Geometric Gothic style favoured by the first generation of British Gothic Revival architects. Stirling and Dewar at any one time had a number of indentured apprentices in their office, one of whom was William Harris, whose Nova Scotia churches are described in the next chapter. In 1869, the year St. Peter's Cathedral in Charlottetown was built to his plans, Stirling, already well advanced in years, found romance in Prince Edward Island in the person of Clara Richmond Lea, whom he married that same year.

There are two outstanding Stirling churches in Halifax: Fort Massey, which was originally Presbyterian and now belongs to the United Church of Canada, and St. David's, which is now Presbyterian but was originally Methodist.

It is unusual for a church to be built on the site of a fort, and unique in Canada. The Fort Massey that gave its name to the church was originally part of the outlying system of fortifications centred on the citadel that protected Halifax on its landward side in its early years, and was named after General Eyre Massey, an Irishman who was commander of the military in Halifax in the 1780s. It overlooked a deep ravine at the end of a ridge that ran northward towards Citadel Hill. It's a steep climb today on three sides to where Fort Massey Church stands, on the site of the old fort. The climb did not deter its parishioners from getting to church, but it did present a problem to the church's third minister, the Reverend Doctor R.F. Burns, a very heavy man. One winter's day, he accepted the kind offer of a youngster to haul him up the icy hill to the church on his sled. They had made it almost to the top when the sled rope broke under the strain, and the good doctor flew back down the hill much faster than he had gone up it.

In the 1860s, there were four Presbyterian churches in Halifax, two of them belonging to The Church of Scotland

Fort Massey Church, Halifax, 1871: interior.

and two to The Synod of the Lower Provinces, and they were in lively competition with one another. The point at issue between them was whether or not a congregation should have the determining say in the appointment of its minister. When Fort Massey Church was opened on the corner of Queen and Tobin streets in December, 1871, it trailed by six months the opening of another new building, also on Tobin Street, built by its south-end Church of Scotland rival, St. Andrew's. Nevertheless, Fort Massey Church flourished. It cost $42,000 to build — a very large sum in those days.

Architecturally, the most notable feature of Fort Massey Church is the variety in the shape, size, and tracery of its

Fort Massey Church: gargoyle. Normally such sculptures adorn waterspouts on exterior surfaces; and because they represent demonic figures they are not often found inside churches.

windows. There are more than a dozen different kinds of windows in the building. Its floor plan is cruciform. The nave is separated from its side aisles by arcades of arches surmounted by a clerestory and enclosed by a hammerbeam roof. Originally, there were two alleys in the nave, each just inside the arcade of piers on either side, leaving a central block of pews that was occupied only by communicants on Communion Sundays, who received the Sacrament from a common cup that was passed from hand to hand and refilled as required by an elder carrying a flagon. This arrangement has since been changed so that now a single central alley runs the length of the nave between the pews, and the Communion is distributed to the communicants in little individual cups. In the front of the church, minister and choristers occupy a platform facing the congregation with the handsome pulpit presented to the church in 1873 in the centre, framed within the great chancel arch and its surmounting label, a Stirling signature. The windows in the aisle elevation on the north side have four-centred arches — so-called Tudor windows — and represent a departure on Stirling's part from his customary adherence to the vocabulary of Geometric Gothic architecture. At the time Fort Massey was being built, William Harris was a seventeen-year-old apprentice in Stirling's office, and must often have spent time at the site, learning from the project. All through his career Harris made constant use of this same shape of arch, in both windows and doorways, the use of which is rare in Stirling's buildings.

Another example of continuity between master and pupil is in the location of Fort Massey Church's steeple — at the corner of the building, rather than in the centre of its end elevation, so placed in order to exploit fully the potential for dramatic effect presented by the church's siting on a street intersection at the top of a hill. This again is a characteristic of Harris's churches. Yet Harris seldom used the threefold portico of which Stirling makes striking use in his design of Fort Massey.

The exterior of Fort Massey Church is executed in an orange coloured brick, with cornices, stringcourses, window and door surrounds, and pinnacles of dressed sandstone. Inside, finely carved foliage and sculptured heads and small creatures adorn capitals and corbels.

Dr. Burns was an outstanding preacher. A capable performer in the pulpit has always been highly prized at Fort Massey. When the church pulpit was vacant, candidates who came "preaching for a Call" were carefully scrutinized, and great care was exercised in the choice of a minister. A contemporary description of the first sermon delivered in 1893 by Dr. Burns' successor, the Reverend Doctor Gandier, emphasizes the pre-eminence of the sermon in the life of a church like Fort Massey:

> Long before eleven o'clock the pews were filled, and standing room was almost gone. Old and young were there. Soldiers and sailors in uniform, students in droves, and large representations from other churches. All the air was filled with the Sunday battery of church bells as the worshippers made their way to taste the new minister. The rich voice, the modest bearing, the perfect articulation ... it was gratifyingly evident that the preach-

er was possessed by an intense but well-controlled enthusiasm, a glowing religious conviction. The boom of the noon cannon on the nearby Citadel, which had always made it necessary for watches to be checked, was not noticed that day as the sermon concluded.[21]

In 1925, the Fort Massey congregation voted 181 to 29 to join the United Church of Canada. Similar margins in favour of church union in the nine other Presbyterian churches in the city and its suburbs left a sizable number of continuing Presbyterians with no church to call their own. However, there was now an abundance of Methodist/United churches, and one of them, the Grafton Street Methodist Church, designed by David Stirling and built in 1869, was sold to the continuing Presbyterians for $30,000.

The Presbyterians renamed the building St. David's Church in 1930; however, the David they had in mind was not the patron saint of Wales, but a David who was King of Scotland in the twelfth century. In 1951, the addition of a church hall necessitated building over part of the Methodist burying ground around the church. The old gravestones were laid flat and the building constructed over them. One stone, that of Mrs. Ann Bell, mother of the fifth mayor of Halifax, Hugh Bell, was moved inside.

St. David's Church, Halifax: exterior elevation on Grafton Street.

St. David's, like many a Methodist chapel in England, has no steeple, but the entrance elevation that rises over Grafton Street, executed in red brick and supported by clustered buttresses topped by pinnacles, is one of the finest architectural compositions in Halifax. A tall, three-light window centres the symmetrical facade above a handsome roofed portico with double doors and traceried transom light. Framed between the corner and the elevation buttresses on either side are upper and lower lancet windows that identify the location of the interior galleries built against three walls of the nave. The fourth wall is pierced by a tall chancel arch very much like the equivalent arch at Fort Massey Church, except that the Fort Massey arch is filled with organ pipes. In 1928, a brick wall that filled in the arch at St. David's was removed and an

Photo by Graham Tuck.

St. David's Church, Halifax: interior, showing the gallery.

which God spoke to Moses in the wilderness) and the X-shaped St. Andrew's Cross, with sprouting buds carved into it to suggest that a tree of sacrifice is really a Tree of Life.

Again on the exterior, the side elevations and the hall addition have a stucco finish. And the small stone heads that greet worshippers as they arrive at the front door are not, as one might expect in a Presbyterian Church, those of John Knox and John Calvin, but those of the Methodist apostles, Anglicans John and Charles Wesley.

Speaking of Anglicans, David Stirling also prepared designs for them. The Hensley Memorial Chapel at King's–Edgehill school in Windsor was built in 1877 as the University of King's College chapel. It is a gem, built of stone in the Early English Gothic style, with slender lancet windows and a large rose window in its west wall. Today it serves the boarding school that

apsidal sanctuary built beyond it against the end elevation of the building. Inside this dignified space, and the linenfold panelling that sheathes the bays of the apse, is accommodated a Communion table, covered by a richly embroidered frontal on which is placed a cross and a pair of candlesticks.

The pulpit, placed to the left of the sanctuary arch, came from Fort Massey's old Church of Scotland neighbour, St. Andrew's, on Tobin Street, and is rich with symbols dear to the Presbyterian heart, such as the Burning Bush (out of

Photo by R.C. Tuck.

Hensley Memorial Chapel, King's-Edgehill, Windsor, 1877.

inherited the King's University campus when it moved to Halifax in the 1920s, but unfortunately the chapel is too small now to accommodate the whole of the school community at the same time. Stirling also designed the nearby King's University Convocation Hall, a Romanesque-Revival-style building built of sandstone that has been splendidly restored in recent years to serve as the King's–Edgehill school library.

Perhaps Stirling's most impressive church is Holy Trinity, Yarmouth, built of brick, with a towered asymmetrical western elevation into which is set a massive window with elaborate Geometric-style tracery. Originally, its tower, now topped by a battlemented parapet, issued in a lofty broach spire. It is sited on a street lined with old trees and some of the handsomest High-Victorian-style dwellings of any town in Atlantic Canada.

Photo by Graham Tuck.

Holy Trinity Church, Yarmouth: exterior.

Chapter Nine
The Harris Churches:
Voluptuous Victorians

DESIGNING CHURCHES WAS THE SPECIALTY of architect William Harris (1854–1913), who although not a native of Nova Scotia (he grew up in Charlottetown in Prince Edward Island), was trained in architecture as an indentured apprentice from 1870 until 1875 in the Halifax office of David Stirling, the immigrant Scottish architect, whom we have already met in Lunenburg, Fort Massey, and St. David's churches in Halifax; the Hensley Chapel in Windsor; and Holy Trinity Church in Yarmouth. Like most first-generation Victorian Gothic Revival architects, Stirling used the Early English and Geometric Gothic styles when designing ecclesiastical buildings. Harris, as a second-generation Gothic Revival architect, was more eclectic, mixing elements from a variety of Gothic periods and places.

The early Harris churches are a High Victorian exercise in the adaptation of medieval English Gothic styles to building in wood in a cold climate. As his knowledge and experience increased, Harris became more and more fascinated by the behaviour of sound in an interior, and found that the architectural vocabulary of French Gothic, with its apses,

unified internal volumes of space, and curved surfaces, served his acoustical purposes better than English Gothic, whose elevations often featured flat surfaces and multiple interior volumes of space that tended to contain sound, rather than distribute it. Yet in the eclectic manner of the High Victorian Gothic Revival architects he continued to pick and choose elements of architectural style from English and Teutonic sources and mix them with the French in creative and highly personal combinations. Thus he continued to use the four-centered, or "Tudor," arch characteristic of the Perpendicular period in English Gothic architecture for windows and doorways in churches that in other respects drew heavily on French Gothic precedents — although he never used Perpendicular-style tracery in any of his windows.

Excellent examples of Harris churches from all periods of his career survive in Nova Scotia, although several have been badly mutilated on the exterior by the application of inappropriate siding materials. This is particularly true of All Saints', Springhill; All Saints', Bedford; Trinity, Sydney Mines; St. John's, Arichat; and St. George's, Falmouth — all

All Saints' Church, Springhill, 1892: exterior as re-clad.

Anglican churches. It was also true of St. Joseph's Roman Catholic Church, North Sydney, until recently, when it was stripped of the vinyl siding that appeared to be damaging its underlying timber fabric after a pinnacle began swaying in the wind. If plastic siding is improperly applied, it can fairly quickly rot a building inside its vinyl wrap.

Shortly before All Saints' Church, Springhill, was built in 1892, Harris had been passed over for consideration as architect of the new cathedral the Anglican diocese of Nova Scotia hoped to build in Halifax. The diocesan authorities seem not to have considered a local architect capable of designing a cathedral, for they had obtained plans drawn by an Englishman, Arthur Edmund Street, son of the prominent Gothic Revival architect George Edmund Street. Harris seems

Photo by Graham Tuck.

All Saints' Church, Springhill: interior.

a large-scale model of what Harris thought a Gothic cathedral in Nova Scotia in the 1890s might be like. Unfortunately, its exterior has been so badly mutilated by insensitive renovation that its virtues are largely hidden under all the kinds of tawdry cladding that have come and gone in fashion over the past seventy years. The church is splendidly situated in the heart of the town, at the top of the hill on which Springhill is built. The Springhill sign that seeks to entice passersby on the nearby highway — "You should see us now!" — could have enhanced meaning should Springhill ever undertake the restoration of the exterior of All Saints' Church to its original appearance. A few old photographs of it exist, and Harris's drawings for it survive in the Confederation Centre Art Gallery and Museum in Charlottetown, that could be used in carrying out a restoration. In any case, much of the scalloped shingling, stringcourses, and belts of board and batten cladding surely survive, together with traces of the original colour, hidden under the later asphalt, aluminum, abitibi board, and vinyl sheathing that has been applied to the exterior of the building from time to time.

to have incorporated elements of his ideas for the cathedral in Halifax into the drawings he prepared for the church in Springhill. Certainly its dignified interior — featuring an arcaded nave flanked by aisles and lit by clerestory windows, full transepts, and chancel terminated by a semi-octagonal partition inside a square exterior — has the monumental character, if not quite the full size, expected of a cathedral. In All Saints' Church, Springhill, Harris was not only designing a church for that town but was also suggesting to the diocese of Nova Scotia that there was no need for it to go abroad to find an architect capable of designing a cathedral.

Nevertheless, All Saints', Springhill, is in itself a gem, quite apart from interesting speculation as to its purpose as

However, no such plea needs to be made on behalf of St. James's Church, Mahone Bay. Just as All Saints', Springhill, is the best Harris church from the period when he was making his transition from English Gothic to French style in the 1890s, so St. James's is the crowning achievement of his earlier English Gothic period in the 1880s.

Mahone Bay has a Harris church because William Harris's youngest brother, Ned, went there as a newly ordained curate to the elderly Anglican rector, William Henry Snyder, in 1884.

Photo courtesy of the Confederation Centre of the Arts, Charlottetown, P.E.I.

All Saints' Church, Springhill: south elevation by W.C. Harris.

Photo by Graham Tuck.

St. James's Church, Mahone Bay, 1886: interior. Its 1887 colour scheme has been preserved through every repainting.

At that time, the Mahone Bay Anglicans worshipped in a fifty-year-old Georgian-style building that shared a hilltop above Bayview Cemetery on the edge of the village with a more recent Gothic-style Presbyterian church. Both buildings were inconveniently sited some distance from Mahone Bay's population centre. When Ned Harris arrived, he learned that the Presbyterians were talking of moving their building closer to where people lived, and that this had alarmed the Anglicans, who feared that some of their more indolent members might be tempted to turn in at the Presbyterian church, rather than travel further to their own, which was too ramshackle to move. But the Anglican rectory was close to the centre of the village on a site large enough to accommodate another building, and there was talk in the parish of constructing a new church there. Between the rectory and the new Presbyterian site was a Lutheran church that had been built some years before. Polite denominational jostling was going on, and eventually it led to the creation of one of Nova Scotia's most familiar streetscapes: three pretty churches standing in a row, their spires reflected in the placid waters of Mahone Bay.

When the time came in 1885 to erect the new St. James's — the last of the three churches to be put in place — the rector, who was active in the Masonic Lodge, wanted to make it a replica of Solomon's Temple in Jerusalem, a Masonic icon. That such a structure might be rather out of place in Mahone Bay seems not to have occurred to him; and one cannot help wondering how he would have attempted to adapt the Temple furnishings appropriate to animal sacrifice to the rituals of The Book of Common Prayer. But the arrival of Ned Harris, whose architect-brother's specialty was churches, put an end to Snyder's dream. Already there were four William Harris churches in Prince Edward Island and one in New Brunswick, and soon it was generally accepted that Nova Scotia would have one too. William Harris would design the new St. James's.

But the project burdened the rector with a further problem. He became convinced that if the local Inglis brothers, one a builder and the other a dealer in building supplies, were engaged as contractor and supplier, the one wealthy man in the congregation, a Mr. Slauenwhite, would refuse his financial support for the project. He feared that a split in the congregation over this issue would spell disaster for the parish and grief for himself in his old age. So, shortly after a start had been made on the new church, he withdrew as

chairman of its building committee and left it in the hands of his young, inexperienced curate. Supported by the women of the St. James's Sewing Circle and by bazaars and garden parties held on the Rectory lawn, the new St. James's was built in two years, within budget, and opened for worship amid great rejoicing on September 27, 1887. Although Slauenwhite did not live to see completion of the building, Snyder's fear that he would withdraw his pledge if Inglis were chosen to build it proved to be unfounded. After Snyder's death in 1889, Ned Harris was elected rector of St. James's parish, and he remained in Mahone Bay until his death, in 1931.

But All Saints' Church, Springhill, and St. James's Church, Mahone Bay, have more in common than their architect. Both reflect the influence exercised in Nova Scotia by Charlottetown's St. Peter's Cathedral, in Prince Edward Island. William Harris was a member of the first class of candidates confirmed in St. Peter's in 1869, and Ned's vocation was nurtured by its first priest-incumbent (as he was styled, rather than rector, because St. Peter's was not a parish church), the Reverend George Hodgson. All Saints' Church, Springhill, was built by the Reverend (later Canon) Charles Wilson, who earlier had taught at St. Peter's Cathedral School in Charlottetown. Both the Harrises and Wilson learned at St. Peter's the principles of the Catholic Revival (or Tractarian Movement) in the Church of England that for fifty years had influenced church architecture and liturgy. In the Maritime provinces, its presence was felt initially in New Brunswick, with the appointment of the first Bishop of Fredericton, John Medley, in 1845, and then in Nova Scotia and Prince Edward

Island with the appointment of Hibbert Binney as fourth bishop of Nova Scotia in 1851. Prince Edward Island was not part of the diocese of Nova Scotia, but an episcopal jurisdiction that had been put in the care of its bishop until such time as it should itself become a diocese. A motion to establish a diocese of Prince Edward Island was passed under Binney's chairmanship by the Island's Diocesan Church Society in 1866, but it had not yet been implemented when Binney, as a first step, made St. Peter's Church in Charlottetown his cathedral in Prince Edward Island in 1879. As such, it would be under his direct control, as was "The Bishop's Chapel" (St. Stephen's) Binney had built in Halifax to promote the Tractarian Movement in Nova Scotia. St. Stephen's stood at the top of Spring Garden Road where it intersects with Robie Street and Coburg Road, on a site occupied today by a small, octagonal bank built of red brick. Binney intended one day to replace it with the cathedral already referred to, built on the same site and complementing St. Mary's Roman Catholic Cathedral at the opposite end of Spring Garden Road.[22] Both St. Peter's and St. Stephen's were intended by Binney to promote by example the sacramental and liturgical "high church" emphases of the Catholic Revival in their respective provinces. The sorts of churches William Harris designed, first in Mahone Bay, and then at Springhill and elsewhere, were exactly what the Catholic Revival called for. Harris served the Catholic Revival in the Maritime provinces in much the same way architects like Scott, Street, Butterfield, Pearson, and Pugin did in England.

Binney's design was only partly successful, perhaps because he died unexpectedly in 1886, before it had been fully implemented. The great cathedral was eventually built in Halifax in 1908–10 by Bishop Clarendon Lamb Worrell, but it was not on Binney's site, and St. Stephen's survived only in the name of a chapel within the cathedral. In Charlottetown, St. Peter's retained the title of cathedral given it by Bishop Binney, but to this day, the Island has not been provided with the diocese or dean and chapter implied in St. Peter's status as a cathedral — although a grassroots movement in that direction developed on the Island in the 1980s and almost succeeded, before it was squelched by the renaming of the diocese of Nova Scotia as the diocese of Nova Scotia and Prince Edward Island in 1999.

Eventually the "high church" impetus that had brought into being churches like All Saints', Springhill, and St. James's, Mahone Bay, slowed, but not before it had had a leavening effect on the Anglican Church in Nova Scotia as a whole that lasted until it began to be replaced by the modernizing influences of the Liturgical Movement and the Second Vatican Council in the Roman Catholic Church. When these began to affect it, the issue mutated into one of traditionalist versus liberationist, rather than catholic versus protestant.

Of course, there were also the other Harris churches, and churches by other architects and builders, that reflected many of the same ideas about the church and worship that were expressed in the churches in Mahone Bay and Springhill. And not all the Harris churches were Anglican. Of the three Roman Catholic churches in Nova Scotia designed by William Harris, St. John's in Windsor is probably the best example of a picturesque building in the province. A small, stone-built, cruciform structure with clerestory and aisles and spired tower, a presbytery house made of wood in the style of a French château is attached to

Photo by Graham Tuck.

St. John's Church & Presbytery, Windsor, 1898: original cladding on the spire has been replaced by aluminum strips that make it seem to disappear on a cloudy day.

it. It was erected in 1898, only three years after Bruce Price had popularized the château style in Canada with his Château Frontenac in Quebec City. St. John's massive sloped roofs, snub gables, dissimilar dormers, two round towers with conical roofs — one rising out of the verandah — combine with a pair of chimneys, the transept gable of the church, and a spired tower to create a slightly fantastic silhouette that defines the King Street approach to downtown Windsor. Unfortunately, the formerly multicoloured shingled spire has been sheathed with bland, off-white cladding

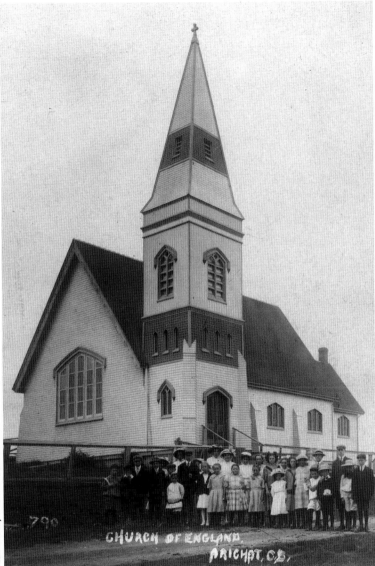

Photo courtesy of the Confederation Centre of the Arts, Charlottetown, P.E.I.

St. John's Church, Arichat, 1895: as it was in the beginning but is not now, having lost its spire and had its exterior sheathed in vinyl.

One of the Roman Catholic Harris churches, The Immaculate Conception, in Truro, was destroyed by fire in 1977. The other is St. Joseph's in North Sydney, built in 1911, a large building of wood capable of seating close to a thousand worshippers in its nave and gallery. St. Paul's in Charlottetown, drawn by Harris in 1894 when he was forty years old, is the first of the churches of his maturity in which a mostly French-Gothic vocabulary is used throughout, and St. Joseph's is among the last. Both have the rib-vaulted ceilings and apsidal sanctuary that contribute to the astonishing acoustic efficiency that made Harris popular as an architect of churches. In St. Joseph's, the original windows, whose Geometric tracery was appropriate in a building in French-Gothic style, have been replaced by windows with English-Perpendicular-Gothic tracery, and stained glass displaying abstract shapes in pale colours. Like St. Paul's and Trinity Anglican Church in nearby Sydney Mines, St. Joseph's has no clerestory, and the broad sweep of the roof of the nave is supported by arcades of piers. The free-standing altar is independent of its matching reredos, and although not by Harris, is well proportioned, and appropriate to the scale of the building.

Several years after St. Joseph's was clad in vinyl siding, one of the pinnacles on top of the tower was seen to be moving in the wind. Subsequent investigation showed wood-rot present in the structure underneath the vinyl, and the vinyl has since been removed and the church reshingled and painted. However, two of the four pinnacles have not been replaced, and the spire has been sheathed in black asphalt roof shingles rather than the textured shingles and banding painted in contrasting but complementary colours provided for in the original design.

that makes it disappear against a cloudy sky; and inside, St. John's has suffered by the demolition of its high altar and reredos, and their replacement by a slab mensa that enables the celebrant to face his congregation from across it, rather like a clerk at a counter serving customers.

St. Joseph's Church, North Sydney, 1911: exterior. Vinyl siding has been removed after the loss of two steeple pinnacles.

Trinity Church, which dates from 1903, also has a gallery — and a finished basement with rooms for Sunday school classes and assemblies. In 1903, the church basement as a place for fellowship, and even secular activities, was a novel-ty among Anglicans, who tended to regard gatherings for purposes other than worship as too profane to take place inside the church, and more properly accommodated in a separate building. But after 1900, Harris's churches more

Photo by Graham Tuck.

Trinity Church, Sydney Mines, 1903: exterior. Vinyl siding still in place.

often than not were designed with basement halls underneath their floors, rather than the crawl space previously provided. The other Harris churches in industrial Cape Breton — St. Alban's, Whitney Pier, and St. John the Baptist, in North Sydney, as well as St. Joseph's — all had finished basements. Unfortunately, St. John the Baptist (Harris's largest Anglican church) was destroyed by fire in 1959, and St. Alban's has been mutilated by inappropriate renovation that includes the replacement of its traceried west window by a cross made of glass bricks.

Trinity Church has also been clad in vinyl siding and, in consequence, has lost something of its character in respect to its external appearance. Whether or not its underlying timbers are being rotted away by moisture trapped under the plastic wrap, one cannot tell simply by looking at it.

However, the vinyl siding is being credited by those responsible for Trinity Church with saving the building from destruction by fire on several occasions: on the walls at the top of the entrance steps, a popular gathering place for unsupervised youngsters, there are smudge marks on the vinyl where cigarette lighters have been held against the vinyl, which has failed to burn.

However, once a building is on fire, siding made of vinyl or aluminum can make getting at the fire to extinguish it more difficult. Copper sheathing on the roof of St. John's Church, Lunenburg, enabled the fire to spread across the length and breadth of the building where the hoses of the firemen were unable to reach it, greatly extending the area of destruction.

The other Harris churches in Nova Scotia are smaller than those in Mahone Bay, Springhill, North Sydney, and Sydney Mines, but for the most part they are articulated in the same French-Gothic vocabulary Harris used after 1894 — although St. John's, Arichat, retains many of the English Gothic features like the squared eastern termination and small chancel familiar from Harris's designs made in the 1880s. St. Andrew's, Mulgrave; St. James's, Newport; St. George's, Falmouth; and All Saints', Bedford are all variations on the same theme, having the unified nave and chancel, apsidal east end, large transept window by the pulpit, nave windows mostly on one side only, groined ceiling, and reredos with niches meant to accommodate statues of saints (usually empty spaces in the Anglican churches, unless occupied by vases of flowers). In several of these buildings, the groined ceiling — an acoustic device — was omitted on grounds of cost. In any case, it was less necessary in a smaller building.

Trinity Church, Sydney Mines: interior. Note the altar painting by Robert Harris.

Photo by Graham Tuck.

In all of these churches a variety of hardwoods is used, and in every building without exception the woodwork is beautifully finished. In the 1950s, St. Andrew's Church, Mulgrave, seemed to its rector, the Reverend Robert Neish, to be much too dark, and so he undertook to make the walls above the wainscotting and in the cells of the rib-vaulted ceiling a light colour. This precipitated a great controversy in the parish, and the congregation divided between those who liked the change and those who didn't. But the change remains, and those who enter St. Andrew's for the first time catch their breath, for being inside this gem of a church is like being inside a jewel.

Photo by Graham Tuck.

St. Andrew's Church, Mulgrave: interior.

St. George's, Falmouth, and St. James's, Newport, were never fitted with the rib-vaulted ceilings that were designed for them, but the quality of their woodwork is the equal of that in Mulgrave. On the exterior, however, St. James's has inexplicably been decked out with a *porte-cochere* that extends out from the umbrage that provides shelter enough around its main entrance. And St. George's has been sheathed in vinyl. Additions to or modifications of Harris churches seldom work well, aesthetically.

All Saints' Church in Bedford — in addition to tawdry siding — has had the misfortune to find itself enclosed in functional but unattractive additions designed to accommodate the various social and administrative functions of a busy suburban parish. Nearly all of its nave windows have been blocked in by the addition of an also nearly windowless parish hall and narthex built against the end elevations of the nave and the hall. When All Saints' was built in 1904, it was to have been with stone quarried on its steeply slanted rocky site, and this intention is reflected in the massive appearance of its squat steeple and fleche, executed instead in wood, and lacking the delicacy of treatment found in equivalent structures in Harris's other wooden churches. Inside, All Saints' is sheathed in dark tongue-and-groove panelling; but it has, nevertheless, something of the same embracing quality and good acoustics that characterize Harris church interiors and make them evocative of the term Mother Church.

The Church of the Transfiguration at Newburn, in Lunenburg County, was built to Harris's plans in 1920, seven years after his death, and lacks the buttresses that would have enriched its exterior appearance. Inside, its tongue-and-groove sheathing has been attacked with paintbrush and light coloured paint, although less successfully than at Mulgrave. Tongue-and-groove boards seldom take paint successfully, and at Mulgrave,

the surface of the boards in the cells between the ribs was covered by flat panels, designed to accommodate the paint reasonably well, which they do.

At Spry Bay, on Nova Scotia's Eastern shore, St. James's Anglican Church was remodelled by William Harris in 1910. He was responsible for the rib-vaulted ceiling rather awkwardly introduced into the building at this time, but the narthex (modelled on that of St. Paul's Church, Charlottetown) and the spirelet added to the ridgeline of the roof are more successful.

St. John's Church, Truro, a handsome stone-built church, the work of architect William Thomas, constructed between 1873 and 1881, had a tower and baptistery designed by William Harris added to it in 1904.

Harris's first church was St. James's Anglican at Herring Cove, drawn in 1872, when he was a teenager learning his craft in the office of Stirling and Dewar in Halifax. It is a small and simple building, with Early-English-style lancet windows adorned with the hood-moulds favoured by his master, David Stirling.

Chapter Ten
All Saints' Cathedral, Halifax:
Holy Hubris

"ONE OF THE CHIEF SEAPORTS of America should, like Liverpool and New York, be marked by the presence of a Cathedral, so that, coming from one country to another, the first thing to catch the eye of the traveller will be that which speaks of the continuity of the Church."[23] So Clarendon Lamb Worrell, sixth Anglican Bishop of Nova Scotia, was quoted in an American architectural journal in 1908 on the subject of his pet project, All Saints' Cathedral in Halifax. Its construction was just getting started, and the bishop fancied it would put Halifax in the same league with Liverpool and New York, where great new Anglican cathedrals — destined to be among the half-dozen largest churches in the world — were just then being built.

But his project was not overly popular in Nova Scotia. Bishop Worrell had recently come to Nova Scotia from Kingston, Ontario, and he was a little pushy. He saw the cathedral as an Anglican status symbol and told his synod in 1906 that it would be a "witness" to "the power of Christianity and the spiritual life in the midst of a material and secular age." Unfortunately for his diocese, what he created turned out to be more like a white elephant.

Nevertheless, the diocese of Nova Scotia has not allowed Worrell's cathedral to get it down. It's still there, still standing — and actually quite handsome. So the cathedral is a triumph, of a sort. It's just that it's not the sort of triumph Worrell intended.

Worrell's predecessor, Hibbert Binney, had left $20,000 towards the cost of building a cathedral — but much more than that would be needed to build it, even in 1887, the year of Binney's death. Years before, he had removed his cathedra, or episcopal throne, from the diocese's original cathedral (St. Paul's, in downtown Halifax) after a dispute, and placed it in St. Luke's, on Morris Street, in the south end of the city. But that was just for the time being. His ultimate goal was to build a permanent cathedral of stone, as Bishop John Medley had done in 1854 in Fredericton. He picked out a spot for it, at the head of Spring Garden Road, where it joins Coburg Road and intersects with Robie Street. As a first step, he put a chapel on the site dedicated to St.

All Saints' Cathedral, Halifax, 1910: cartoon for All Saints window.

Stephen, which he operated as an Episcopal peculiar, using it to promote Tractarian ideas, much as he had been doing in Charlottetown since 1869 with St. Peter's Church. He envisaged Spring Garden Road becoming a kind of axis on which Halifax would turn, with cathedrals at either end, St. Mary's Roman Catholic Basilica with its granite spire at the lower end near the harbour, and the new Anglican cathedral with its complementary steeple at the higher end, right in the very centre of the peninsula on which Halifax is built.

It was a neat idea, but it was completely lost on Worrell. After St. Luke's was destroyed by fire in 1904, it was clear that the time had come to build the cathedral. But Worrell abandoned Binney's site at the top of Spring Garden Road and chose instead a site with a rivulet running through it midway between Binney's chapel and St. Luke's: the old Halifax exhibition ground on Tower Road. He described it as a compromise site between the other two churches, but he may have wanted to erase the tradition Binney had established at St. Stephen's.[24] He already had a set of plans for a cathedral that had been sitting around since 1887, drawn by Arthur Edmund Street, the son of George Edmund Street, one of the leading lights of the Gothic Revival in England. They were shown to William Harris, who had already designed many successful churches for the diocese in places like Mahone Bay and North Sydney, and was a devout Anglican, as well. Harris had dreamed all his life of seeing a great cathedral built in Halifax, and had submitted his own plan for it in 1887. He advised against using Street's design on the grounds that it was not suited to the Nova Scotia climate, and offered to prepare new plans for the project himself. His offer was accepted, and he produced drawings for an acoustically efficient stone-built church seating twelve hundred. Its most promi-

nent feature was a single steeple placed in the centre of the exterior end elevation of the nave, clearly conceived to dominate the view up Spring Garden Road — even though the cathedral now would more likely be built facing the park between Tower Road and South Park Street.

Bishop Worrell took Harris's plans to Toronto, where they were criticized by his clergy friends. They didn't like the single steeple set against the end elevation of the nave, even though their own cathedral, St. James's, had the same configuration. They thought the tower should be at the crossing, as in English cathedrals like Salisbury. To them Harris's proposal looked more like a parish church than a cathedral. So they advised Worrell to go to the prestigious New York architectural firm of Cram, Goodhue, and Ferguson for a design. When Harris heard this he was upset, and sought out members of Worrell's building committee, showing them documents attesting to his standing as a Canadian architect. But his Canadian testimonials failed to impress the committee. "If Harris is any good, why is he still in Canada, in Halifax?" seems to have been their attitude.

So the bishop got new plans drawn in New York by Bertram Grosvenor Goodhue, done in the same Perpendicular Gothic style Goodhue had used for the new Graduate School at Princeton, the chapel at the West Point Military Academy, and the 5th Avenue, New York, Presbyterian church — all very prestigious buildings. And his cathedral had a central tower at the crossing, like Canterbury and Gloucester and the new cathedral being built in Liverpool. It looked like a cathedral. But how was the diocese to get out of its obligation to Harris? The building committee decided to ask him to nominate an arbiter to choose between his design and Goodhue's. Harris agreed, and nominated Percy Nobbs, the professor of design at

McGill University in Montreal. He didn't know Nobbs personally, but he'd read speeches Nobbs had made in which he'd advocated the development of a Canadian architecture and spoke favourably of the Arts and Crafts Movement, both enthusiasms that Harris shared. But Nobbs opted for Goodhue's design, and was scathing in his criticism of Harris's drawings, which were made on watercolour paper, as if they were more art than architecture. In a further concession to Harris, his firm, Harris & Horton, was entrusted with the supervision of the work of building Goodhue's cathedral when its construction got underway in 1908. This fell to Harris's partner, William Horton, who supervised all the firm's work in the city of Halifax.

By 1906, when the choice between Goodhue and Harris was made, Harris's High Victorian Gothic style was beginning to look a little dated. Perpendicular Gothic was much more fashionable, and Cram, Goodhue, and Ferguson were its leading practitioners in North America. In retrospect, the popularity of Perpendicular Gothic in the early years of the twentieth century represents the twilight of the Gothic Revival that dominated Victorian times. It had, of course, originated in England late in the Middle Ages, and is characterized by the use of four-centred, or Tudor, arches in doors and windows and vaults. These arches make possible wide openings in the fabric of a building, so that windows can be made wide and admit lots of light. In southern European climes, as for example in Italy and Spain, Gothic windows are narrow, in order to keep interiors dark and cool. In the cloudy north, as in England, there is less light, and it is therefore the more valued. The building in which the large windows made possible by the four-centred arch are accommodated becomes, essentially, a framework of stone filled with walls of glass. Perpendicular churches also often feature fan-vaulted ceilings set over lofty naves and aisles. Goodhue drew All Saints' Cathedral in this style with huge east and west windows, major and minor transepts, and a nave flanked by low processional passages under a triforium topped by very tall and wide clerestory windows. The cathedral was built in just two years, 1908–1910, but the end bay of the seven bays of the nave, the end elevation facing Tower Road, the central tower, and the vaulted ceiling called for in Goodhue's plans were not built. They were left until later, and now are unlikely ever to be built, except for the permanent stone-built end elevation. It was constructed to new plans by Allan Duffus in 1979, Goodhue's original design for the elevation having been considered too costly to implement.[25]

Goodhue's design is undoubtedly handsome, and it is easy to understand his popularity as an architect in the Perpendicular Gothic style. On the other hand, his design for All Saints' Cathedral suffers from a serious functional disability that was immediately apparent to William Harris. Its flat wall surfaces, and the interruption in the roofline occasioned by the central tower, created acoustical problems that Harris's design avoided with its apse, unbroken roofline, and rib-vaulted ceiling. Harris had made a study of acoustics that prompted him to abandon the vocabulary of English Gothic architecture in favour of the French, which was less angular and more unified, voluptuous, and curvaceous. He even drew a diagram in an attempt to explain the acoustical superiority of his design in comparison with that of Goodhue. But Worrell does not seem to have been overly concerned with the

All Saints' Cathedral, Halifax: Allan Duffus's west front, 1979.

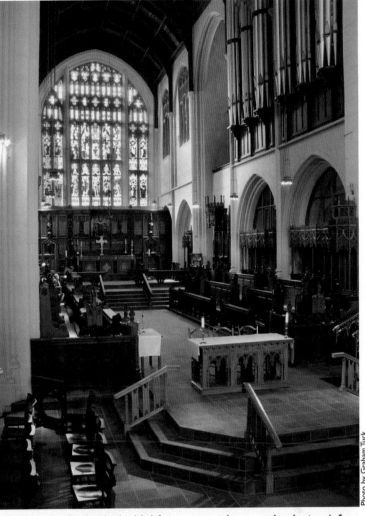

All Saints' Cathedral, Halifax: nave altar and choir (after Hurricane Juan).

acoustical or liturgical efficiency of the building. What he had his heart set on was an Anglican status symbol.

But for many years, concern for how well the cathedral functioned acoustically and liturgically was overridden by other concerns having to do with the quality of its construction. If Bishop Worrell and his committee had adhered to the specifications Goodhue provided with his plans, many of these troubles might have been avoided. But Worrell was determined to get as much for his $127,000

budget as he could. And he wanted the cathedral ready for the scheduled meeting of the national general synod of the Church of England in Canada, to be held at Halifax in September 1910.

The contractor engaged for the project was S.M. Brookfield, a Nova Scotia firm, and the contract was signed on December 20, 1907. The form of contract employed was a standard one, recommended by the American Institute of Architects. Article 3 read, "No alterations shall be made in the

All Saints' Cathedral, Halifax: nave and font.

work except upon written order of the Architect". This was scratched out and replaced by a clause reading, "The owner shall have the right to order that portions of the work under the present contract shall be changed, added to or omitted." This opened the way for the use of cheap materials and building techniques in the construction of the cathedral. In 1929, Percy Nobbs noted that "brick was changed to rubble of low grade, or to reinforced concrete, plaster was substituted for cut stone, wood was substituted for concrete."[26] When it rained, it was discovered that the cathedral was far from watertight. The cellar, which a parishioner described as "like the underneath of a wharf," was constantly filling with water, perhaps partly because it had been built over the bed of a small stream, but also because the concrete stone used extensively in its buttress caps, window and door surrounds, and window mullions was not watertight. Almost from the day of its opening, the cathedral began to disintegrate.

Beginning in 1918, and over the years that followed, many studies were made of the building and various remedies attempted to halt its decay. Consultants named Brown and Dyer reported that the mortar used had not been properly mixed and recommended pulling it down and rebuilding it. In 1919, Worrell (who was now an archbishop) invited Goodhue to come to Halifax at Worrell's expense to see the cathedral and advise on its restoration and maintenance. Goodhue admitted that in his designs there was an absence of "drips" from "unmoulded weatherings" but that any water that got into sills and buttresses made of the "concrete stone" that was used ought to have been stopped by the copper or lead underlays he had specified. If these were missing it must have been "either by direction, or permission, of Messrs Harris and Horton."[27] He declined the Archbishop's invitation to visit Halifax, and appears never to have seen the cathedral he had designed.

There were mutterings in the diocese that Harris and Horton, disgruntled at losing the commission, had botched the building of the cathedral on purpose. Harris had died in 1913 (in 1910 he suffered the first of the heart attacks that killed him shortly after the cathedral was opened), and it remained to Horton to defend their reputation, which he did vigorously, claiming, for example, that he had used more copper flashing than Goodhue had specified and that the mortar had been correctly mixed. He wrote, "the walls admit so much water the mortar has suffered from water and frost

all these years so that it has been seriously affected." He considered that it had been a mistake to use so much "concrete stone" instead of the more expensive dressed stone called for in the specifications.

In 1929, Percy Nobbs was called in to look at the cathedral. He reported, "What must now be corrected is the result of certain errors of judgement in design with respect to climate."[28] For this, of course, Goodhue was responsible. But Nobbs was not prepared to find the design of the cathedral to blame for its disintegration, for it was on his recommendation that Goodhue's design had been chosen. He focussed his blame on Horton — who, like Harris, was now dead — chiefly for not keeping detailed records of the departures that had been made from Goodhue's specifications. Nobbs consulted Goodhue's plans and specifications, but he did not find them to be of much use as a guide to what had actually been built. Nevertheless, Archbishop Worrell got off lightly: Nobbs wrote, "In All Saints' Cathedral you have a building with a superb plan involving a fabric which demanded a much higher expenditure than you have made upon it."

As far as the general public was concerned, the Halifax Explosion of 1917 — and the later explosions in the Bedford Basin Ammunition Magazine in 1945 — were invoked as having contributed to the woes of the cathedral. But whatever the spin put on the problem by the ecclesiastical authorities, the Anglican parishioners of Nova Scotia rallied to the cathedral's cause. Architect Arthur Wallace, whose father, a retired bank manager, toured the parishes as a fundraiser for the cathedral, wrote, "At that time money happened to be plentiful from the rum-running and bootleg trade. The result was fantastic. I believe something like $300,000 odd was collected in cash during the summer of

1929 or '30, near the beginning of the Depression." That was twice what the cathedral had cost to build in 1908.

If the money that has been poured into propping it up, then and since, had been budgeted into its initial construction, and a longer time taken to build it, there would have been no need to cheapen its construction. After all, the Liverpool Cathedral, begun in 1904, took seventy years to build, and St. John the Divine Cathedral in New York is not yet finished after one hundred years.

The visitor to All Saints' Cathedral today is made little aware by what he sees of the agonies the building and those who minister in it and from it have gone through. The great "east" window faces west, and so does not glow in the morning light when congregations are largest, but its perpendicular panels are filled with splendid figures of angels and archangels and all the company of heaven ranged in glory around the throne of Christ. Below it, the oak reredos and choir stalls are richly adorned with figures of more saints and angels. The choir is flanked by St. Stephen's Chapel on one side, where the weekday offices and masses are said, and in a columbarium chapel on the other, where the ashes of many who have served in the lay ministry of the cathedral are interred. One of the great transept windows shows the consecration of Charles Inglis in 1787 as the first bishop of Nova Scotia, and above it, the descent of the Holy Ghost in tongues of flame on the Apostles on the Day of Pentecost is vividly portrayed. A new "west" window, designed by John Burden, shows Jesus preaching from a boat; it and the shore and the crowd occupy only the lower portion of the window, with the rest of the space left blank, as if to suggest the fog that blankets much of the Atlantic shore of Nova Scotia. Through it, light pours into the nave of the cathedral from the back, where the flat concrete and plaster walls, once cement-grey, and stained by streaks of lime leached out of the mix from which they'd been made, are now brightly and cheerfully cream-coloured. It's the sort of space that lifts spirits; and if it is a little difficult, even with the good electronic amplifying system installed in the cathedral, to hear everything that's being said or sung, All Saints' Cathedral, after close to a hundred years, has a firm place in the affections of Nova Scotia Anglicans.

Postscript: After this chapter was written, on September 29, 2003, Hurricane Juan struck Halifax and inflicted considerable damage on All Saints' Cathedral, so that the building had to be closed for some time while repairs were made. Bishop Frederick Hiltz, in a letter addressed to the parishes of the diocese written a few days later, described what happened when the storm struck:

> The flat roof over the tower at the transept crossing blew off! About two and one half tons of wood frame, roofing material and copper flashing were hurled into the Nova Scotia Rehab Centre parking lot behind the Cathedral. Also significant portions of the shingled roof over the chancel blew off. With the heavy early morning rain the chancel and transept areas were flooded. Within hours the Dean, Cathedral wardens, and a number of other members of the Cathedral congregation worked hard to cover the altar, chancel stalls, the organ and other valuables in the Cathedral.

Chapter Eleven
Les Églises Acadiennes à Chéticamp et Clare: Gallic Grandeur

Nova Scotia's Acadian population is descended from approximately one hundred families who settled mostly in the western and eastern ends of the Annapolis Valley in the seventeenth century. They built dikes and farmed the lush meadowlands that border the Minas Basin. By the middle of the eighteenth century, when they became caught in the bitter wars between France and England, there were more than ten thousand Acadians. After they refused to take an oath of allegiance to King George in 1755, the English, to whom title to the mainland of Nova Scotia had been ceded by France in the Treaty of Utrecht forty years earlier, decided to expel them. Although the Acadians were French and wished to remain so, they also desired to be neutral in the conflict between England and the mother country that had abandoned them. But their refusal to accept the rule and religion of the English made the British military nervous. Were they really neutral, or were they just biding their time until Paris should show some concern for them? It was still not safe for people in the fledgling settlements at Halifax and Lunenburg to venture too far into the sur-rounding woods, for some who had done so had been killed by the Mi'qmaq allies of the French. Governor Lawrence decided that the Acadians would have to go. So the English herded some of them onto ships and resettled some of them in small groups in their New England colonies and attempt-ed to return others to France — although many died when two of the ships foundered in an Atlantic storm. Small num-bers of Acadians managed to escape into the woods or made their way to northern New Brunswick where they were hunted down by Colonel Robert Monckton (thousands of Acadian descendants live today in the New Brunswick city named after him), or to Quebec City — which fell to the English in 1759. There seemed to be no escape for the Acadians from the British, save for a few who got to the tiny islands off Newfoundland, St. Pierre et Miquelon, that remain the property of France to this day.

However, in 1762, Massachusetts refused to accept a shipload of Acadian deportees, and in 1764 the British changed their policy and allowed the Acadians to return to Nova Scotia. By this time their former lands had become

Photo courtesy of College Ste-Anne.

L'Église Ste-Anne du Ruisseau, Yarmouth, 1900: exterior.

occupied by others, and in founding new settlements in Nova Scotia (as they now had to refer to Acadia) they were not allowed to live in large groups, but in small settlements separated by Anglo communities. Today's Nova Scotian Acadian communities date from this period, and are scattered around the province's perimeter — at Pomquet, Chéticamp, Isle Madame, Port Felix, and Charlos Cove, and the Clare district between Yarmouth and Digby — with Anglo settlements in between.

Perhaps it was because earthly kingdoms had proven so unaccommodating to them that the Acadians relished, more than most people, their citizenship in Heaven, and reflected that attachment in the magnificence of the churches they built. For this they have been criticized over the years by their Anglo neighbours, who cannot understand why the Acadians should build such magnificent churches and live themselves in what are mostly rather modest dwellings. Apart from the fact that there is often more than a little envy in such criticism, the Acadian can suggest to his Protestant neighbours that they too could

have a really nice church if they had not broken themselves up into so many denominations.

The recovery of the Clare Acadians of western Nova Scotia from the upheaval and dislocation of their expulsion and return was greatly enabled by the leadership of a thirty-six-year-old priest named Jean-Mandé Sigogne who came to them from England in 1799. He had been ordained in the diocese of Tours in France in 1787, but had been forced — with thousands of others who refused to submit to the demand of the republic established by the French Revolution that they swear allegiance to it, rather than to the Pope — to find friendly refuge in England in 1792. During the seven years Sigogne spent in England, he directed a small boarding school, sold books, tutored the daughters of a wealthy lady who taught him English, worked as a cooper, and adopted an orphaned Irish girl, providing for her education. But he was eager to return to the exercise of his priesthood, and when presented with the opportunity to do so among French-speaking people in Nova Scotia, he accepted it gladly.

He was sent to a settlement near Yarmouth called Ste-Anne du Rusisseau. His biographer, Gérald Boudreau, says there were:

> ... practically no roads, the villages small, dispersed and isolated one from the other, with communication between them only possible by sea or through forest. The people were poor, the economy elementary and modest; the daily enterprise of the average family meant scrabbling out a basic sustenance through domestic farming and fishing. The

housing was simple, for the most part log cabins with one room…[29]

The people had been without a priest for a long time, and they were uninstructed in religion and lax in morals. Three months after his arrival he had drawn up a set of articles designed to regulate social and religious behaviour, and had persuaded no fewer than seventy-two heads of families to sign it under oath. In 1803, he administered the oath of allegiance to King George III to his parishioners at the request of the Governor, Sir John Wentworth; and in 1820, after receiving help from his successor, Sir James Kempt, following a devastating fire in Clare, he described himself as being "under a double obligation of gratitude to the benevolence of the English people. I had first experienced it, with many French Ecclesiastics, not without admiration, when the terrible and cruel Revolution forced me to take refuge in England."

When he died in 1844, the *Yarmouth Herald* noted, "He was esteemed by all classes, and by men of all religious denominations; as a peace-maker he was almost proverbially known; his charities were boundless; the poor houseless wanderer of whatever creed, the untutored Indian or hapless African, found in this worthy man present relief and every provision he could make for their future welfare."

He built nine churches, including one for Mi'kmaw people, whose language he learned, at Bear River, and the predecessor of the present Église Ste-Marie at Church Point. Boudreau notes, "The admiration and esteem given to this man who remained steadfast and faithful to God and to his priestly calling is not surprising."

L'Église Ste-Marie, Church Point, 1905: exterior.

L'Église Ste-Marie at Church Point is the largest wooden church in North America, and perhaps in the world. It was built in just two years, between 1903 and 1905, by a carpenter named Leo Melanson, who could neither read nor write, but was able to understand the French architect's

Photo courtesy of College Ste-Anne.

L'Église Ste-Marie, Church Point: interior.

plans. In its spirit and proportions it's a Gothic building, although executed in neo-Classical style, with round-headed windows and hip roofs on the transepts. The tower is topped by a spire that reaches 185 feet into the sky. Incredibly it was once even higher, at 212 feet, but lost 27 feet after it was struck by lightning in 1916. The steeple tends to sway in the wind, so thirty-six tons of rock have been deposited in it to act as ballast. The church's floor plan is cruciform, 190 feet in length, with generous transepts 135 feet wide, a clerestoried nave, and a lofty apse that rises to a height of close to 70 feet beyond the high altar. For all that it is so large, it is essentially a simple building in concept and rather plain in its shingled, unornamented exterior.

On its western side is the four-storey-high main building of St. Anne's College, built in 1899, the only Acadian university in Nova Scotia, designed by William Harris, and adorned with dormers with snub gables and sloped sides like those on houses in Normandy.

L'Église St-Bernard, St. Bernard: exterior.

Very different from L'Église Ste-Marie is St. Bernard's Church, a few miles east of Church Point, construction of which began in 1910. Blocks of granite were quarried near Shelburne, on the other side of the province, and brought by train to St. Bernard, where they were unloaded into ox-carts and brought to the site. This went on for thirty-two years until the church was finished and consecrated in 1942. It has twin towers that flank its entrance elevation, bold transepts, and an apsidal altar wall.

But the grandest of the Acadian churches is l'Église Saint-Pierre at Chéticamp, on Cape Breton Island. It is the fourth church to serve the community, which was established in 1785 when a group of deported Acadians made their way back to their homeland from exile. Their first church was built of logs,

97

Photo courtesy of Collège Ste-Anne.

L'Église St-Bernard, St. Bernard: interior before construction of transepts and apse.

in a back district called Belle Marche, but it was replaced in 1812 by a wooden church dedicated to St. Apollinaire. This was, in its turn, succeeded in 1861 by a church built of stone, this time perched on a hill between Belle Marche and Chéticamp harbour, that could be seen for miles around. It was a symbol of the emergence of the Catholic Acadians from their long night of rejection in their own native land.

In 1875 the Reverend Pierre Fiset came to Chéticamp as parish priest. Over the next thirty-four years, until his death in 1909, Father Fiset made an immense impact on the community. He established a model farm, developed the fishery, got a grist mill and a sawmill into operation, and even put people to work mining and processing gypsum. But his major project was the new l'Église Saint-Pierre.

Saint-Pierre is the sort of spectacular church one sees in Quebec, its silver-coated spire rising above the roofs of its town or village along the banks of the St. Lawrence River. That's not surprising, in view of the fact that its architect

L'Église Saint-Pierre, Chéticamp: exterior.

Although the spirit of l'Église Saint-Pierre, Chéticamp, is clearly Baroque, its vocabulary is largely neo-Classical.

The local general merchant, Robin, Jones, and Whitman, looked after getting the stones with which the church is built quarried on nearby Chéticamp Island. They were hauled across the ice on horse-drawn sleds. The church is 212 feet long and 74 feet wide. Its steeple, 180 feet high, is placed in the centre of the western gable. Inside, the nave is galleried on three sides, with a Casavant organ made in 1904 above the entrance.

Elizabeth Pacey, in her 1983 book on Nova Scotia churches, *More Stately Mansions*, described the interior of l'Église Saint-Pierre as probably "the most highly ornamented in the province." She wrote:

> ... three levels of arches, the wide arches at ground level, the classical rounded arches of the side galleries, and the smaller recessed arches along the central ceiling arch, provide an inspiring rhythmic beauty. Everywhere there is rich embellishment, from the gilt-touched scrolls on the pillar capitals and the deeply moulded cornice work to the intricately patterned gold medallions which surround the gallery lights.

was David Ouellet of Quebec City, and that the contractor responsible for its construction was Hubert Morin of Trois-Pistoles, Quebec. In fact, everything that went into it in the way of furniture and finish also came from Quebec.

David Ouellet (1844–1915) was, in his day, Quebec's leading architect, and designed close to eighty churches. Like his contemporaries elsewhere, he adopted an eclectic approach to architectural styling, but tended to be more conservative in his mix of architectural elements than the Anglo-American High Victorian Gothic and Romanesque Revival architects.

A low, wrought-iron screen extends across the entire width of the church, dividing the sanctuaries of the high altar and the side altars from the nave. A flight of seven steps inside the screen leads between two ambos to the high altar. It stands at the top of the traditional three steps provided for the celebrant, deacon, and sub-deacon at High Mass —

99

although now Mass is celebrated more usually in the manner ordained by Vatican II by a celebrant (with concelebrants) from behind a communion table set below the subdeacon's step. Yet the sumptuous reredos behind the high altar survives, with a life-sized statue of St. Peter standing within it under a canopy. Surely when the Chéticamp parishioners arrive at the Pearly Gates they will find themselves on familiar ground!

L'Église Saint-Pierre, Chéticamp: interior.

Photo by Graham Tuck.

Chapter Twelve
St. Ninian's Cathedral, Antigonish:
Gaelic Grandeur

Bishop Colin MacKinnon, the third Bishop of Arichat, initiated the building of a new parish church in the rising town of Antigonish in 1866, but it was called a cathedral from the beginning, as if everyone knew that the seat of the bishop would be moved eventually from Arichat to Antigonish. Bishop MacKinnon had spent nine years in Rome, and he wanted a Roman-style basilica in Antigonish. The plans drawn by a Quebec architect named A. Levesque were adopted, Bishop MacKinnon turned the first sod on October 22 of 1866, and the hauling of stone from quarries outside town on horse-drawn sleds continued through the winter. On May 16, 1867, a stonecutter named Ronald MacGillvray signed an agreement with Bishop MacKinnon and the rector of the parish, the Reverend Hugh Gillis, to build the foundation and the walls up to the window ledges. The cornerstone was laid on June 29, 1867, the Feast of St. Peter and St. Paul. The church took seven years to build, but it wasn't until 1886, when the name of the diocese was changed to the diocese of Antigonish, that St. Ninian's officially became its cathedral.

St. Ninian, like other early British saints, is a shadowy figure. The son of a Cumbrian chieftain, he is described by the venerable Bede as having gone to Rome as a youth, where he was eventually consecrated bishop (probably by Pope Siricius) in 394. En route back to Scotland, he ran into St. Martin of Tours (famous for having shared his cloak with a beggar), to whom he later dedicated the church he built at Whithorn in Wigtownshire as a centre of evangelism in north Britain. The church was called Candida Casa, meaning White House, no doubt because of its colour — built either of white stones or white-washed. Ninian's fame as an apostle of the Scots, as well as his lengthy sojourn in Rome (so much like Bishop MacKinnon's) would have commended St. Ninian to the bishop as an appropriate choice as patron for the new church in Antigonish that one day would be the diocesan cathedral.

No doubt the move of the seat from Arichat, an Acadian community, to Antigonish, a Scottish settlement, was a sensitive one; but Arichat, on Isle Madame, was not geographi-

Photo by Graham Tuck.

St. Ninian's Cathedral, Antigonish: exterior.

cally convenient, either for the residence of the bishop or for the location of the college named in honour of St. Francis Xavier that Bishop MacKinnon's predecessors had started there. MacKinnon moved the college, as well as his episcopal seat, to Antigonish. Indeed, the cathedral today is set in the midst of the college buildings, just as Ninian's monastic community in the Celtic world of fifth-century Britain would have been clustered around his Candida Casa. What Bishop MacKinnon and those who came after him created in Antigonish was, therefore, no new thing. They followed a pattern inherited from Celtic antiquity, in which the house of God is set in the heart of the community, rather than

Photo by Graham Tuck.

St. Ninian's Cathedral, Antigonish: interior.

apart from it, so that the spiritual life might penetrate and freshen the whole life of its inhabitants in a natural way.

The man who built St. Ninian's was also a Celt, but Irish — Sylvester O'Donoghue, a native of County Wicklow, in Ireland. Atop the entrance facade of the finished cathedral there is an elevated pediment containing an empty niche (meant to be occupied by a statue of St. Ninian?) and the words in Gaelic *TIGH DHE*, meaning "house of God." On one side is a carving of a thistle, the Scottish emblem; on the other, the Irish shamrock — Celtic symbols on a Roman basilica.

St. Ninian's is built of limestone and sandstone with a roof of slates imported from Scotland, and is 170 feet long

St. James's Church, Antigonish, 1862: exterior.

and 70 feet wide. Inside, stairs ascend within the twin towers to a gallery that accommodates the organ and choir. At the sanctuary end of the building, a baldacchino supported on just two columns extends out from the wall behind the high altar. Originally, there was a large, Romanesque-style window in this elevation, but it was filled in when a sacristy was built against its exterior in 1937. The baldacchino covers the sedilia provided for the celebrant and his deacon and sub-

Lion and Lamb sculpture, St. James's Church, Antigonish.

Photo by Graham Tuck.

deacon, rather than the altar, which stands free in the Vatican II manner in front of the baldacchino. There is an arcade of Corinthian columns supporting a series of Romanesque arches that march down both sides of the nave, dividing it from high processional passages on either side and the exterior side walls, each side with its rhythmic series of nine tall round-headed windows set under circular oculi, each pair framed within a Baroque trim. The ceiling is flat, and on it are four Gospel scenes — the Nativity of Christ, His Crucifixion, His Ascension, and Christ as the Good Shepherd — all painted by Quebec artist Ozias LeDuc. The Stations of the Cross on the nave walls also take the form of oil paintings on canvas, and are the work of LeDuc or his students. On the walls above the arcades are near-life-size fresco portraits of the Twelve Apostles, plus St. John the Baptist and St. Cecilia.

St. Ninian's seats fifteen hundred, and cost £40,000 to build. Its bells were cast in Ireland and were "baptized" in the names of saints Ninian, Joseph, Columba, and Margaret

of Scotland. It has no crypt, but Bishop MacKinnon is buried in a vault under the sanctuary.

There are two other churches in Antigonish that are worthy of notice. St. James's United Church (formerly Presbyterian), a large wooden building in the main street, has Gothic fenestration, but its proportions and trim are Georgian. It was built in 1862, and is a good example of how people accustomed to Classical style in architecture attempted to accommodate themselves to the Gothic style when it reasserted itself in the middle of the nineteenth century, by making windows and doorways pointed, rather than rounded, yet at the same time retaining familiar Georgian-style proportions. The steeple, set saddleback-style on the roof above the front elevation, has an octagonal belfry that sits on a square pinnacled tower and is surmounted by a slender spire.

St. Paul's Anglican Church, on the other hand, a much smaller building, was built forty years later, and is thorough-

St. Paul's Church, Antigonish, 1902: exterior.

Photo by Graham Tuck.

ly High Gothic Revival in its proportions as well as in its details. It was designed by Gustavus Bernasconi, a member of the congregation, and recalls in its asymmetrical elevations, colour, and richness of cladding texture churches in his native Switzerland.

The widespread notion that religion encourages violence is denied in Antigonish, where a remnant of the trunk of an elm, victim of Dutch elm disease, has been refashioned into a lion and a lamb lying together in peace in front of St. James's Church.

Chapter Thirteen
Star of the Sea, Canso:
Cradle of Co-op

ON THE EASTERNMOST POINT OF the mainland of North America, jutting out into the Atlantic at the end of a long and winding road, sits the small and unimportant-looking Nova Scotia town of Canso. But appearances are deceiving. Much has happened here. As long ago as 1604, native Mi'kmaq traded with Basque fishermen at Canso, and it was here that the first Catholic mass in Acadia was celebrated, by Father Biard, in 1611. Early in the next century, the mainland of Nova Scotia became a British possession, but in 1718 a visitor reported that Canso was "peaceable and quiet, the French and the English fishing with all friendship and love."[30] That changed as Britain and France duelled with each other through the eighteenth century. In 1720, the French and their Mi'kmaq allies destroyed the New England fishing station at Canso, and the British responded by sending soldiers to Canso and building a fort. A town grew on Grassy Island in Canso harbour, with well-appointed two-storey houses, and in 1735 a school with fifty pupils was in operation under the direction of the Reverend James Peden, an Anglican missionary. In 1744, a French detachment from Louisburg came and burned the settlement and carried off its inhabitants, later releasing them. The next year, a New England force returned to Canso and used its harbour as a staging area for a successful assault on Louisburg. Under the peace treaty that followed, Louisburg was returned to France and Britain replaced the lost settlement at Canso by founding Halifax, in 1749. When Canso eventually did recover, it was not on Grassy Island, but on the mainland side of the harbour, and it was not until the late twentieth century that archaeologists established the substantial nature of the eighteenth century settlement.

The land of the peninsula on which Canso was perched was bleak and infertile, but the waters into which it thrust were full of fish. There was wealth in the sea, but its rewards tended to accumulate in the hands of a few buyers and merchants and suppliers of gear to the fishermen. Most of the fisherfolk were of Acadian and Celtic stock, with a sprinkling of the descendants of Hessian soldiers given land in Guysborough County after the American War of Independence in the 1770s. Many were illiterate and poor and, except for the Hessians, mostly Roman Catholic. The earliest church built in the new Canso

Photo by Tom Kavanaugh.

Star of the Sea Church, Canso, 1885: exterior from the harbour.

on the mainland side of the harbour was the Roman Catholic Star of the Sea, in 1845, which was replaced by the present building in 1885, after a fire. The part of the town around it was known as Irishtown. Later, Canso became an almost cosmopolitan place, with Western Union and Commercial Cable company offices with large staffs, and churches belonging to the Baptists, Methodists, and Anglicans.

In 1891, Pope Leo XIII issued his famous encyclical *Rerum Novarum* that marked the beginning of the emergence of the Roman Church from the defensive stance it had adopted in reaction to the Reformation in the sixteenth century and the Enlightenment in the eighteenth to engagement with the modern world. The purpose of *Rerum Novarum* is described by *The Oxford Dictionary of the Christian Church* as:

to apply to the new conditions created by the Industrial Revolution the traditional Catholic teaching on the relationship of a man to his work, profit, masters and servants. On the ground that society originated in the family, it proclaimed private property a natural right and condemned socialism as infringing it. It upheld wage settlements by free agreement, the rightfulness of combinations of workers or employers, and above all the idea of a just wage, defined as "enough to support the wage earner in reasonable and frugal comfort" with a family. It maintained that the natural place of women was in the home. It also emphasized the duty of the state to preserve justice and the responsibility of the Church in the moral aspects of employment.

Nevertheless, socialist regimes, ideologically based in the dialectical materialism of Karl Marx, became established in a number of powerful states in ancient Christian lands and in the Far East. But as the twentieth century ran its course, *Rerum Novarum*'s condemnation of socialism was vindicated by socialism's failure, a failure that became more and more evident toward the century's end. The world had followed the wrong prophet in dealing with the problems attendant upon industrialization. Marx's jibe that religion was the opiate of the people and Stalin's contemptuous question, "How many divisions has the pope?" epitomized the twentieth century's vain pursuit in the wrong direction of what turned out to be a red herring of massive proportions.[31]

A humble priest named Jimmy Tompkins, vice president since 1908 of St. Francis Xavier College in Antigonish, Nova Scotia, was concerned about many of the same issues that *Rerum Novarum* addressed. In 1912, he attended a British universities' meeting at Oxford in England that triggered in him a passion for adult education as the key that would open the way to a better life for the poverty-stricken rural people of eastern Nova Scotia: how would they otherwise ever be able to acquire the knowledge and the skills necessary to look after themselves in their relationships with those who dominated and exploited them? He instituted adult education extension programs at St. Francis Xavier designed to relate learning to life, within a Catholic context, in a practical way.

But it was not this, per se, that got him banished to Canso in late December, 1922. It was his support for the Carnegie Corporation of New York's scheme for a federation of the sectarian universities of Nova Scotia that would be centred on Dalhousie University in Halifax. To the Bishop of Antigonish, this looked like a secularizing threat to the Catholic identity of St. Francis Xavier University. But Father Tompkins had no doubt but that Catholic scholars in fields of learning from Astronomy to Zoology would be able to hold their own with Protestants and Atheists and any other ideologues they might encounter in academia.

At the end of the day, the only university that moved into association with Dalhousie was King's College in Windsor, grasping at its only hope of survival after the destruction by fire of its main building in 1921 — a promised donation from Carnegie that was contingent upon its rebuilding on Dalhousie's Studley campus in Halifax, rather than in Windsor. Baptist Acadia remained in Wolfville, Methodist Mount Allison in Sackville (just over the border in New Brunswick), and Roman Catholic St. Francis Xavier in Antigonish. Contrary to the Carnegie design, they remained unaffiliated with one another.

In Canso, Father Tompkin's altar was now that of Stella Maris, or Star of the Sea Church, a lovely, but conventional, wooden church in Gothic style that had been built there in 1891 by

Star of the Sea Church, Canso: archival photo of the interior.

Sylvester O'Donoghue, a native of County Wicklow in Ireland, who earlier had supervised the crew that built St. Ninian's Cathedral in Antigonish. Stella Maris, unlike St. Ninian's, is in Gothic style, and consists of a six-bay nave, with a low tower set into its western elevation topped by a slender spire. On the eastern elevation, there is a large sacristy. Inside the church, a gallery with a curved front dominates the back of the nave, and a rib-vaulted ceiling supported by arcades of arches springs from piers on either side of the nave. The nave has six bays, boldly defined by buttresses on the exterior, each

with its own window. There are many churches in eastern Nova Scotia like it, but Star of the Sea (as Father Tompkins preferred to call it, rather than the Latin Stella Maris) is special, in that it is set so neatly among the houses "over the hill," as they say in Canso, its reflection sparkling in the waters of the harbour between the mainland and Grassy Island — that is, when the fog is not in and the sun is shining.

In Canso, Father Tompkins seemed to be about as far removed from Antigonish and the university scene as he could possibly be. Nevertheless, he set about putting his

Photo by Tom Kavanaugh.

Star of the Sea Church, Canso, after Vatican II. The old altar and reredos have been replaced by a plain free-standing altar table, set below a cross and a banner. The two statues that once occupied niches above the altar now stand on the foor, flanking the celebrant, who stands behind it facing the people (when he is not seated, as in the photograph). The communion rail has disappeared, and communicants now receive the Sacrament standing.

ideas into practice at the parish and community levels. He was particularly successful in the Acadian settlement of Little Dover, near Canso, which was described as so poor that it had only one cow that gave milk (many families in the small settlements that clung to the rocky Atlantic shore kept a cow as a matter of course in order to provide their children with fresh milk each day).[32] By 1934, in the depth of the Depression, Little Dover had a credit union, a co-op store, and a debt-free fishery co-operative. The programs of adult education, and the credit unions and co-operatives, that Father Tompkins had set into motion from Antigonish continued. He remained in Canso until 1934 when, after a brief spell as hospital chaplain at Antigonish, he served St. Joseph's Parish in Reserve Mines in Cape Breton Island from 1935 until his retirement at the age of seventy-eight in 1948.

When I arrived in Canso as rector of All Saints' Anglican parish in 1956, I had no knowledge of Father Tompkins or of the town's long history. I remember being greeted by the Sisters of St. Martha (whose presence in Canso was another of Father Tompkin's achievements) with the gift of a home-baked pie. Several years later, I was asked to take part in a symposium titled "The Church and the Atlantic Economy" put on by the Anglican diocese's Council for Social Service in Halifax. I was the first speaker, and was given five minutes to describe what economic conditions were like in a Nova Scotia fishing community. Later speakers talked about the coal mines, the steelworks, manufacturing, the farming sector, and there was a keynote speaker. Last of all, the premier, the Honourable Robert Stanfield, took the platform, ignored everything that had been said by all the other speakers, and lit into me because I had bewailed the plight of the inshore fishermen. He said that before the war the (Roman Catholic) parish priest in Canso had successfully circulated a petition among the inshore fishermen to keep the fish companies from acquiring the large draggers that at that time were the wave of the future in the fishing industry. In consequence, the fish companies, prevented from modernizing their operations, had pulled out of Canso. This, he said, was why the fishing industry in Canso and the people that depended upon it were in a precarious situation.

After the meeting I went back to Canso, where the only fish processing plant in operation at that time was British Columbia Packers, a private firm that had come in during the Second World War, but which had recently announced its intention to pull out of Canso. The Co-op plant that dated back to Father Tompkins' time in the 1930s was not functioning, due to management problems that had lost it its market. The only co-op venture that was continuing to operate was a grocery store. I related the story of my encounter with Premier Stanfield to friends in the co-op, and they said that what he had said about the petition and the companies leaving was substantially correct.

Under the leadership of a retired cable station employee named Bill Windeler, a member of the Canso Baptist Church, we then formed a community development association that worked hard to re-establish the economic viability of Canso based in the fishery. With the assistance of Mr. Stanfield's government, Acadia Fisheries was brought in, and a magnificent new fish-processing plant was built, with its own fleet of trawlers. Never in its history had the future looked more promising for Canso! But long before the new plant was built, I had been moved to Halifax, and in my place in 1970 was the Reverend Ron Parsons, a Newfoundland fisherman's son. With the new plant and the trawlers and their crews, there also arrived in Canso the United Fishermen and Allied Workers' Union, headed by Homer Stevens, a communist. Before very long, the UFAWU went on strike, and Canso descended into a nightmare of strife and violence.

Now, thirty years later, the Atlantic fishery has collapsed, the new plant is closed because it has no quota of fish to process, and the economic outlook for Canso is bleak. The resource was mined — destroyed by greedy men who failed to understand or accept the stewardship principle enunciated in the Gospel the churches exist to serve. Father Tompkins had gotten it right: the fish were in the sea to feed families and support communities, not to make money for a few or to empower protagonists in a class war.

Chapter Fourteen
First United, Truro:
Ironic Icon

THE UNITED CHURCH OF CANADA came into being on June 10, 1925, but it was just the last step in a long process. Both the Methodists and the Presbyterians, the two principal partners in forming the United Church, had achieved unions of their own towards the end of the nineteenth century — mending rifts that had splintered the Methodists into Bible Christians, Wesleyans, Primitive Methodists, Calvinistic Methodists, etc. — after they had broken with the Church of England in 1795, and the Presbyterians into several sorts of synods that, as we've seen, competed with one another in Halifax. Buoyed and exhilarated by their success at stitching their separated parts together, many of the leaders of both the Methodist and Presbyterian churches began looking beyond their own traditions for new partners with whom to unite. After all, the Lord had prayed that all His followers be one.

Logic might suggest that the Methodists in their search for such a partner would have cast their eyes first at the Church of England because that was their mother church. But mothers and daughters do not always get along very well, and that was certainly true of the Anglican–Methodist relationship throughout the nineteenth century. The *London Daily Telegraph* put a finger on the problem in its publication *AD, 2000 Years of Christianity,* published as a newspaper supplement to mark the start of the third Christian millennium in 2000, when it noted that John Wesley had set out to strengthen the Church of England; instead, he founded a new denomination: Methodism. All across the Anglophone world throughout the nineteenth century Methodist chapels and churches sprang up everywhere and drew people from older religious persuasions, as well as from among the unchurched.

So the Methodists looked at the Presbyterians and found them much more attractive than the Anglicans. One of the attractions was that the Presbyterians were like themselves, in that they didn't have bishops and didn't much care for them, either. So the courtship of the two denominations got underway. It lasted twenty years, and in some places — like romances today — the partners were so eager to get

First United Church, Truro, 1913: exterior, front view.

Photo by R.C. Tuck.

Photo by Graham Tuck.

First United Church, Truro: exterior, rear view.

together that they didn't wait for the knot to be tied. In the town of Middleton in the Annapolis Valley, for example, the union of the Methodists and the Presbyterians was consummated in 1923, two years before the actual union of the two denominations took place in 1925. So, to this day, the United Church of Middleton is proud of having been a Methodist–Presbyterian love child.

But, alas, there was not love everywhere. Consider the town of Truro, "the Hub of Nova Scotia," as its residents call it, certainly the hub of Colchester County, which until 1925 was almost as Presbyterian as Pictou County next door. On Truro's main street is a large and handsome church built of brick, with a steeple in Renaissance style that would not look out of place in Sir Christopher Wren's London — or perhaps

Photo by Graham Tuck.

United Church, Middleton, 1877: exterior.

I should say the London of the Scottish brothers, architects Robert and James Adam. The sign in front identifies it as First United Church. Next to it is a somewhat smaller, but just as handsome, church built of stone in the Gothic style. The sign in front identifies it as St. James's Presbyterian, and its cornerstone carries an inscription that says it was built in 1928.

There is no hint in the architecture or the siting of these two buildings that they represent a dispute or a difference of opinion or a hurt of any kind. There is no wall between them. Neither church is host to a wooden figure carved from the trunk of a dead elm tree such as may be seen all over Truro, striking a hostile or defensive pose toward the neighbouring building.

Of course, there may never have been a time when these Christians did not love one another. But around about 1925, some of them did find it difficult, for prior to 1925 First United Church was First Presbyterian Church. After church union, instead of the number of churches in Truro having been reduced by one, there was actually one more than there had been before. Across Canada close to 100 percent of the Methodists voted for church union, but only 70 percent of the Presbyterians did. In Truro, the First Presbyterian congregation voted 611 in favour, 43 against. A second Presbyterian church in the town, St. Andrew's, voted 122 to 55 in favour. Both formerly Presbyterian churches are United Church of Canada churches today, and as the United Church of Canada across the country views itself as the legitimate continuation of the pre-union Presbyterian Church, so First United and St. Andrew's United see themselves as continuous with pre-1925 First Presbyterian and St. Andrew's Presbyterian in Truro.

So where does that leave St. James's Presbyterian, built next door to First (ex-Presbyterian) United in 1928? Which of the two is the legitimate heir to the Presbyterian church built in Truro in 1767 by the fifty-three Scottish immigrant families who in 1760 were settled on the lands vacated by the Acadians expelled in 1755 — the only church in the community until 1821?

The ninety-eight persons in the two Presbyterian congregations in 1925 that voted against church union represented a sizable minority, and so they got together and formed the St. James's Presbyterian congregation that in 1928 built the new, Gothic-style Presbyterian church alongside the former First Presbyterian Church that now was the First United Church of Truro. The pain and hurt went deep, but the new building, designed by J.G.W. Campbell, Truro's town engineer, and patterned on the former Presbyterian Church in Kentville, Nova Scotia (now the United Church of

Photo by R.C. Tuck.

First United and St. James's Presbyterian churches, Truro.

St. Paul & St. Stephen), became a source of comfort for those to whom church union had been a nightmare.

Lucy Maud Montgomery, whose famous fictional heroine, Anne of Green Gables, was an orphan, and whose husband, the Reverend Ewen MacDonald, was a Presbyterian minister, eloquently expressed the feelings of the orphaned Presbyterian minority about church union when she said, "From all points of view, I think it is a tragic blunder. The stately Presbyterian Church, with its noble history and inspiring traditions, has been forced to commit Suicide."[33]

In the 1960s and 1970s a similar church union scheme designed to knit together the United Church of Canada and the Anglican Church of Canada came to the brink of commitment when the Anglicans pulled back. It was those old Anglican villains, the bishops, who stopped it. The hymn book and the liturgical forms created by the planners and

Photo by R.C. Tuck.

The People's Church, Truro.

designers of the proposed new church had been published, and many Anglicans judged them to be inferior to what they already had in their books of Common Prayer and Common Praise. An archdeacon in the diocese of Ontario reflected the general opinion that if the union scheme went forward, one-third of Anglicans would go along with it, one-third would not, and one-third would drop out of church life altogether. The bishops were close to their people, and were not prepared to put them through what the Presbyterians had gone through fifty years earlier.

So the goal of church union remains elusive. In the Truro area (the last time we looked) there were twenty-eight churches: First United Church, St. Andrew's United Church, Brunswick Street United Church, St. James's Presbyterian Church, Immaculate Conception Roman Catholic Church, St. John's Anglican Church, St. George's Anglican Church, Abundant Life Victory Church, Calvary Pentecostal Church, The United Pentecostal Church, Central Nova Wesleyan Church, The Church of the Nazarene, Cornerstone Assembly Church, First Baptist Church, Truro Heights United Baptist Church, Zion United Baptist Church, Immanuel Baptist Church, Grace Independent Baptist Church, Crossroads Baptist Church, Glenwood Christian Church of Christ, John Calvin Christian Reformed Church, the Nova Scotia Agricultural College Christian Fellowship, the Shepherd's Heart Prayer Centre, The Seventh-day Adventist Church, The Salvation Army, The Truro Alliance Church, The Vineyard Christian Fellowship Church, and The People's Church — founded by radio evangelist the Reverend Perry Rockwood, minister of St. James's Presbyterian Church from 1944 until 1947, when he was excommunicated by the Halifax-Lunenburg Presbytery of the Presbyterian Church and took with him some part of St. James's congregation.

In the Middle Ages, towns in Europe the size of Truro had as many churches as Truro, Nova Scotia, has today, but all of them would have been Catholic, in communion with one another in the same diocese, and supervised by the same bishop.

Chapter Fifteen
First Baptist, Halifax:
Anglo-Cool?

WHEN THE REVEREND JOHN TWINING, erstwhile curate and would-be rector of St. Paul's Church, Halifax, was made Garrison Chaplain, the dissidents who had followed him out of St. Paul's were left as sheep without a shepherd. Gradually, many of them found their way into St. George's Round Church congregation. But about twenty remained, and they came under the influence of another former Anglican, the Reverend John Burton, whose congregation consisted mostly of black people. In 1827 this group invited Dr. Ira Chase, of the Newton Baptist Theological Institute in Massachusetts, to come to Halifax to help them organize a Baptist church in the Nova Scotia capital. On the morning of September 30, 1827, Dr. Chase baptized several of the new Baptists in Bedford Basin and in the afternoon a stone chapel on Granville Street that had been obtained by Mr. Twining's supporters (thinking that it would eventually become an Anglican Church) was opened as the Granville Street Baptist Church. The Reverend Alexis Caswell, whom Dr. Chase had brought with him from Massachusetts, remained behind as its first minister.

Baptists are advocates of "believers' baptism" and, as such, reject the notion that the baptism of infants, practised by other churches, makes sense. They point out that in the New Testament persons are baptized upon profession of faith, which can only be made by an adult, not by an infant. And they say, again citing New Testament precedents, that baptism ought to be by immersion, rather than by pouring or affusion. Early Baptists were persecuted, which helped increase their numbers. *The Oxford Dictionary of the Christian Church* says that Baptists in modern times "trace their origins to the actions of John Smyth, a Separatist exile in Amsterdam, who in 1609, reinstituted the baptism of conscious believers as the basis of the fellowship of a gathered church," and describes them as "pioneers in pleas for freedom of conscience and religious liberty."

The new Baptists were leading citizens of Halifax, and well-educated men and women. Their stability and intellect, together with the spiritual fervour of those who had been caught up in the emotion and vitality of the New Light revivalist movement that had swept rural parts of Nova

First Baptist Church, Halifax, 1950: exterior on Oxford Street.

Photo by Graham Tuck.

Scotia earlier, provided the Baptist Church in Nova Scotia with remarkable depth and staying power. In 1838, the members of the Granville Street Baptist Church played a leading role in the founding of Acadia University in Wolfville, Nova Scotia, not far from Windsor, where Bishop Charles Inglis's Anglican King's College continued to strug-

gle to maintain a precarious existence, as it had since 1789.

In the course of time, the congregation of the Granville Street Baptist Church outgrew its premises, and in 1886 a new church was erected at the corner of Queen Street and Spring Garden Road on a site that had been purchased in 1870, and on which a schoolroom had already been built in

First Baptist Church, Halifax: interior from the gallery.

Photo by Graham Tuck.

1875. At the same time it was renamed, becoming the First Baptist Church of Halifax. On March 21, 1942, it was destroyed by fire, and for eight years the congregation met in St. Andrew's United Church Hall on Coburg Road, a building that now belongs to Dalhousie University.

There was some question whether or not First Baptist would rebuild, but rebuild it did, this time at yet another new site, on Oxford Street near the western end of South Street, across from the Dalhousie University campus. The new church, drawn in the English Perpendicular Gothic style by architect Bruce Brown of Toronto, was dedicated on April 16, 1950.

Anglican Theology students, who lived at the other end of the block at the University of King's College (now relocated to Halifax after its Windsor building had been destroyed by fire in 1921), were among those who were fascinated by the new Baptist church and paid it regular visits as it neared completion. This was because it looked so Anglican. Newspaper reports described it as patterned on an English parish church. Its floor plan was cruciform, with nave and chancel and transepts. Arcades of slender piers ranged chastely down both sides of the nave, separating it without either triforium or clerestory from the side elevations, with their towering windows filled with Perpendicular tracery and plain opaque glass. At the chancel steps, pulpit and lectern flanked a central alley dividing cantoris and decani stalls. The Communion table stood altarwise before a dorsal curtain that hung within a frame above a retable, on which stood a cross flanked by two candlesticks. The curtain enclosed a baptismal tank for the administration of baptism by immersion. Inside the entry on Oxford Street, a narthex extended the width of the building and provided access on either side to dignified stairways leading to a gallery with a sloped floor extending back to a tall tower window filled with glittering stained glass. The church is an immaculate product of the late, late Gothic Revival. It was all paid for within two years, and in 1958 extensive schoolrooms and social facilities were added to the building, all in styling congruous with that of the church, constructed in the local dark-grey ironstone with dressed sandstone facings and window surrounds.

In 1921 First Baptist Church made a momentous decision: it extended "Fellowship Membership, without immersion," to those "of other denominations who wished to join" the congregation.[34]

Chapter Sixteen

St. George's Greek Orthodox, Halifax:
The East comes West

EASTERN ORTHODOXY CAME LATE TO Nova Scotia, but it is now very much part of the religious landscape in the seaside province. Orthodoxy is similar to Anglicanism, in that its constituent national churches are autocephalous, or self-heading, and are organized on a territorial basis into dioceses headed by bishops in communion with the ecumenical patriarch, the patriarch of Constantinople who, like the archbishop of Canterbury among the bishops of the Anglican Communion, is accounted the first among equals with a primacy of honour, rather than of jurisdiction. While Orthodox priests normally are married, Orthodox bishops are not, for only monks are eligible to serve in the episcopal office. There are two Orthodox churches in Halifax: St. Anthony's Antiochian Orthodox Church, whose congregation derives mostly from the Levant and worships in a Gothic-style building on Windsor Street that has undergone several metamorphoses, and St. George's Greek Orthodox Church, whose congregation moved, in 1977, from the old St. Luke's Anglican Church Hall on Morris Street, where it had been since 1941 (and had transformed the interior of a very Anglo, brick-and-sandstone, Gothic-Revival building of 1863 into an outpost of the mysterious East with icons and screens and flickering lamps) to a new site at Melville Cove on the Northwest Arm, where it built first a basement schoolroom and hall in 1977, and then, on top of that, a splendid new church of brick in the Byzantine style in 1983.

This was an accomplishment achieved not without difficulty. As often happens in churches undertaking building projects, there were sharp disagreements, even "cruel words" (or so the parish history says), as church members debated the pros and cons of a new facility. Nor was it easy to find in Halifax an architect who understood the Byzantine style. By this time, in the 1970s, the Greek community in Halifax had grown to more than 250 families, and at great festivals the little church on Morris Street was so crowded that sometimes congregations overflowed onto the sidewalk. A move to a more spacious site was urgently needed — but where? Two sites near the Morris Street church and another on Inglis Street were considered and rejected. In 1975, a three-and-a-half-acre site at Melville Cove became available when a developer who

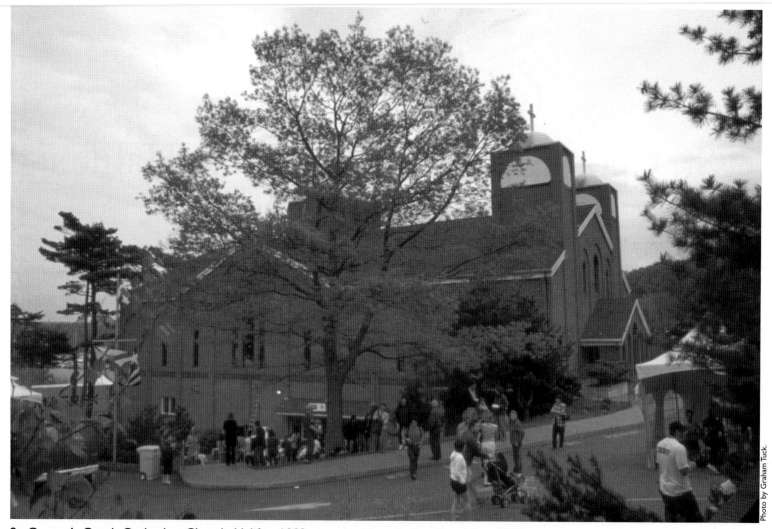

Photo by Graham Tuck.

St. George's Greek Orthodox Church, Halifax, 1983: exterior view during Greekfest, 2003.

had acquired it with the intention of building a motel on it was unsuccessful in having it rezoned for commercial use. The church paid $161,000 for the property, and within two years, despite the disputes, erected on the site a community centre at a cost of $360,000. The money was raised and the building paid for within four years, allowing construction of the church on top of the new structure to proceed. St. George's congregation did not allow the differences of opinion, sharp as they were, to frustrate the success of the project. On January 28, 1984, a dome made of fibreglass was lowered into place, and the new church became a reality.

What would Anthemius of Tralles and Isidore of Miletus, the architects employed by the Byzantine Emperor Justinian in creating the dome that floats over Santa Sophia in Constantinople, have thought of making a dome of fibreglass and lowering it into position by means of a crane? But that is what Halifax architects Dumaresq and Bryn did. The achievement of the Halifax architects may not be compara-

Photo by Graham Tuck.

St. George's Greek Orthodox Church, Halifax: interior.

ble with that of Justinian's pair, even though Santa Sophia's first dome fell in soon afterwards and had to be rebuilt. But St. George's does nevertheless "incorporate Byzantine features of architecture" (as the official history of the church puts it) even though it may not be classic in every respect.

Greek Orthodox churches normally are square in their floor plans, based on a Greek cross, the arms of which are of equal length — although often an attached narthex conveys the impression that the interior is longer than it is wide. A dome, representing Christ, spans the interior space and dominates the exterior of the church, and four smaller domes (although St. George's has only two), usually on short towers at the four corners of the building, represent the four Evangelists, Matthew, Mark, Luke, and John, and their Gospel witness to Christ. Inside, across the front of the church, is the iconostasis, or screen on which the icons are

125

hung. Behind the screen, like Heaven itself, is a realm of mystery, where the altar is placed. In an Orthodox church what you see is not all you get. At St. George's, a gallery extends across the back of the church, and in it is accommodated the iconostasis from the old church on Morris Street. It's a link with the old building, now made into apartments, for which warm affection is slow to fade among the members of Halifax's Greek community.

Vignettes

One: Yarmouth Cathedral

Photo by Graham Tuck.

ST. AMBROSE CATHEDRAL, YARMOUTH, NOVA Scotia, became a cathedral when the Diocese of Yarmouth was carved out of the Archdiocese of Halifax in 1953. It is one of several churches designed by George Henry Jost (1852–1922), a descendant of George Jost, a blacksmith, one of the "Foreign Protestants" who came to Halifax in 1750. George was a founder of "The Little Dutch Church" on Brunswick Street — where he is reputed to have made the rooster weathervane that still sits atop its steeple (see page 44). George Henry was also architect of the third St. Peter's Church in Dartmouth (the first was a small wooden building that stood at the foot of Spring Garden Road in Halifax until its removal across the harbour to Dartmouth in 1830, when St. Mary's Cathedral was erected on its site). St. Peter's, Dartmouth, bore a strong family resemblance to St. Ambrose's, Yarmouth, for both churches were about the same size, and constructed of red brick in a neo-Romanesque style. St. Peter's was destroyed by fire three days after Christmas in 1966.

Local craftsmen contributed to the construction of St. Ambrose's Church: Richard Carroll built the foundation, Fraser Gavel did the masonry, Ambrose Porter the carpentry, and James Murphy the painting. Ste-Anne-du-Ruisseau Church, just outside Yarmouth, a wooden building erected in 1900, is similar in its neo-Romanesque style to St. Ambrose's Cathedral, although built of wood rather than brick; but Ste-Anne's even closer similarity to St. John the Baptist Roman Catholic Church in Springhill, Nova Scotia, suggests that J.C. Dumaresq may have been its architect.

Two: Unidentified Flying Object?

Photo by Graham Tuck.

Bear River boasts that it is "The Switzerland of Nova Scotia" because it is such a hilly place, having been built on the sides of a ravine that cuts through the western end of the ridge that defines the southern side of the Annapolis Valley. In the nineteenth century, Bear River was a great shipbuilding place, and home to skilled carpenters who could build a church as well as a ship. In 1859, they constructed a church for the Bear River Baptists with a steeple that looks more like what one might see at Kiev, Ukraine, or perhaps in Lombardy, Italy, than in Nova Scotia. The name of its architect is unknown.

The body of the church is conventional Gothic Revival in style, but as the building works its way up to its steepled extravagance, the cornice on the elevation against which the steeple is set abandons restraint and launches itself on a course of voluptuous curves that prepare the eye for the outburst above.

The dome on the cupola is 14.5 feet in diameter and 6 feet high in the centre. The original dome was replaced in 1968 by one built of fibreglass in Mahone Bay by a maker of fibreglass boat hulls. The men of the church installed it in one day, and employees of the manufacturer used to sealing boats were on hand to make sure its four sections were watertight. It is lighted at night, and the sight of it floating above the treetops has given rise to reports of flying saucers hovering over Bear River.

Three: Simon Gibbons's Churches

Photos by Graham Tuck.

The Reverend Simon Gibbons was the son of an English sailor and an Inuit mother, born at Red Bay, Labrador, in 1853. He was brought up and educated by Edward Feild, Anglican bishop of Newfoundland. He served in parishes in Nova Scotia, where he demonstrated remarkable skills both as a designer of churches and as a raiser of the money needed to build them. His signature as

Reverend Simon Gibbons, once rector of this parish and principal collector of the funds which built this church, was born in Red Bay, Labrador in 1853 and died rector of Parrsboro, N.S., in 1896, the result of an injury received when he saved from death two ladies whose carriage was about to be dragged over the cliffs by runaway horses. The font in the church is Saxon carved and 1200 years old. August 1928

an architect is a tower with a helm roof, as in the example above: Holy Trinity Church, Jordan Falls, with its double-helm roof. Simon Gibbons's last parish was at Parrsboro, where he built another church with a helm-roofed tower, St. John's at Diligent River. Other Gibbons churches with helm-roofed towers are St. John's Church, Baddeck, and St. Mark's Church, Moose River, near Parrsboro. On one occasion, he travelled twenty miles on snowshoes, there and back, to take the Sacrament to a sick parishioner at Spencer's Island. He died in 1896 in consequence of injuries he received when he "saved from death two ladies whose carriage was about to be dragged over the cliffs by runaway horses."

Four: Crousetown Crafty

Photos by Graham Tuck.

Sᴛ. Mᴀʀʏ's Cʜᴜʀᴄʜ (ᴀʙᴏᴠᴇ) ᴡᴀs a schoolhouse prior to 1914, when a handful of Anglicans living in the minuscule village of Crousetown in the backwoods of Lunenburg County bought it at an auction with the intention of making it into a church. There was a Methodist church in the village already and the Crousetown Anglicans didn't think their chances of getting the building would be very good if their Methodist neighbours suspected they wanted it for a church, so they got some Anglican friends in the neighbouring village of Petite Riviere to bid on it at the auction. They were successful, and so Crousetown today has two churches — and not many more houses than that. In recent years the interior of this simple church has been enriched by many acquisitions: an old font from St. John's Church, Fairview; a paschal candlestick carved by Dennis House; an organ built in London, England, in 1826; an altar triptych carved by Colin Starnes, former president of the University of King's College; an iron screen wrought by Michael Spencer; and a Blessed Sacrament House made by Eric Conrad. The stained glass windows are by Robert Wikstrom. A lectern and the rose window came from a demolished church at nearby Italy Cross. To the right of the door by the altar is a memorial to Gottleib Crouse, who married the daughter of Cornwallis Moreau, reputed to be the first baby born in Halifax, and the son of the first missionary to Lunenburg, the Reverend Jean Baptiste Moreau. His descendant, the Reverend Dr. Robert Crouse, long-time professor of classics at Dalhousie University, has made St. Mary's Church into a popular venue for concerts and recitals, and is the individual primarily responsible for its transformation into a treasure house of ecclesiastical arts and crafts.

Five: The Church of All Nations

THE CHURCH OF ALL NATIONS on Robie Street in Halifax originally had a much more limited dedication, as The J. Wesley Smith Memorial Church. It grew out of a Methodist mission on nearby Charles Street and was built to a design by Charles Hopson in 1902. Most of the cost was met by a local businessman, J. Wesley Smith, who died shortly after he assisted at the laying of the cornerstone on August 4, 1902. In the years following the First World War it had a congregation of more than one thousand people and was reputed to have the largest Sunday School in the Maritime provinces. In 1925 it became, like all the Methodist churches, part of the United Church of Canada. In recent years demographic changes in the north end of Halifax led to the United Church turning it over to

the Christian Reformed Church Halifax congregation, which had been sharing the building with its United Church owners for several years.

The Church of All Nations is a fascinating building architecturally. It is octagonal in shape, and set in its roof is a lantern with twenty-eight small Gothic windows, several of which are filled with clear glass placed so that beams of sunlight will fall at certain times on a painting of an open Bible on a wall to the left of the platform occupied by the choir and the preacher. One is reminded of six-thousand-year-old Stone Age burial mounds in Britain built so that a beam of sunlight shines in the entrance of the tomb and penetrates into its deepest part at the winter solstice.

Photos by Graham Tuck.

Six: Be Fruitful and Multiply

IN THE ANNAPOLIS VALLEY TOWN of Berwick the United Church (left) and Christ Church Anglican (right) sit side by side. Christ Church is the older of the two buildings and has had an eventful history, having been erected originally at Grafton, several miles east of Berwick c.1854, and then moved into Berwick when Berwick grew and Grafton didn't. It was a small building in the Early English style, with a bell-cote rather than a steeple, and lancet windows and corner boards on the outside and dark tongue and groove paneling on the interior. Wesley Methodist Church (later United), erected in 1857, had a larger congregation. The Methodists also owned and operated the nearby Berwick Campground — a twenty-five-acre site with ninety cottages and other buildings under towering pine trees that drew many hundreds of campers to evangelistic programs every summer (and still does). But in 1938 Wesley Church was destroyed by fire, and two years later its replacement was erected next door to Christ Church. Not everyone was pleased when the rector of Christ Church, invited to preach at one of the dedicatory services in February 1940, congratulated its congregation on coming and "nestling alongside the dear old Mother you left 150 years ago."

But since then Christ Church itself has had a facelift: a new front elevation was put on the building in 1993, and a

Photo by Graham Tuck.

mini-steeple replaced the bell-cote on the roof — although the square tower on the United Church next door (hidden by a tree in the photograph) is more impressive.

Berwick boasts itself "The Apple Capital of Nova Scotia." The varieties of apples grown in the Annapolis Valley orchards have counterparts in the varieties of churches. One of the varieties of apple was developed by Charles Inglis, whom we met on his farm at Clermont, between Aylesford and Middleton: it is called the Bishop Pippin.

Seven: Exotica in Whitney Pier

Photo by Graham Tuck.

WHITNEY PIER, A DISTRICT ON the east side of Sydney, the Cape Breton metropolis, beyond the site of the now dismantled steel works, boasts one of the richest ethnic mixes in its population of any community in Canada. Ukrainians, West Indians, Poles, Lebanese, Italians, and Gaels drawn by the prospect of work in the mines and steel mills of industrial Cape Breton made their homes in Sydney and found themselves subject to racial discrimination as well as toxic contamination. But the members of each group found fellowship among their own kind in their churches. In Whitney Pier there are Catholic congregations that worship in Polish, Ukrainian, and Italian, as well as in English. Whitney Pier may have a bad image because of the nearby Sydney Tar Ponds, but it is a community of clean streets and neat neighbourhoods.

Shown here are Holy Ghost Ukrainian Catholic Church, with its onion-shaped dome and cupolas (left), and St. Philip's African Orthodox Church, with its slanted roof and unique outdoors picnic area, where a Caribbean Festival has been held each year since 1983. The Ukrainian Catholic Church has its roots in the western Ukraine, where, under Polish influence, it split in 1596 from the Ukrainian Orthodox Church and placed itself under the authority of the Bishop of Rome while retaining its Eastern liturgical tradition. The African Orthodox Church, on the other hand, represents a movement towards Orthodoxy on the part of a group of immigrant blacks, some of them Anglicans from the West Indies who did not feel comfortable in the local Anglican church.

Eight: Academically Correct

THE BAPTIST AND ROMAN CATHOLIC Churches may be thought to be at opposite ends of the Catholic-Protestant divide in Christendom, but the chapels built to accommodate each tradition on the university campuses in Wolfville (Acadia) and Antigonish (St. Francis Xavier) in Nova Scotia share the same neo-Classical Georgian or Colonial style. The St. Francis Xavier Chapel was built in 1948 and seats 650 upstairs with room for an additional 700 in a basement auditorium. Its Stations of the Cross were made by a hard-rock miner turned artist, Angus MacGillvray. The Acadia Chapel, designed by Harold Wagoner of Philadelphia, is smaller, and was built in 1960–63. Its unusual stained glass windows, symbolic of God as Father, Son, and Holy Spirit, and made by Henry Lee Willett, undergo subtle changes as light conditions vary.

The King's College, Halifax, and Universite Ste-Anne, Church Point, chapels are also neo-Classical in style, with its lineage from Greek architecture. The use of this style for academic chapels suggests that Nova Scotia's educational institutions, with their roots in churches, see no conflict between reason and revelation.

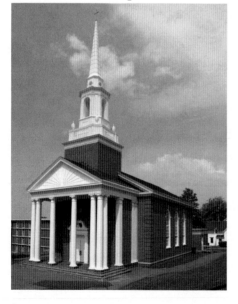

Acadia University's Chapel (left, and above bottom) and the St. Francis Xavier University Chapel (above top) are each dedicated to the memory of alumni: Acadia's Fred C. Manning and St. Francis Xavier's Dr. John E. Somers.

Nine: Upon This Rock...?

Anglican Church
Rawdon N.S.   17ᵗʰ Aug 1912 RH

Dᴿɪᴠɪɴɢ ᴛʜʀᴏᴜɢʜ ᴛʜᴇ ᴡᴏᴏᴅs ʙᴇᴛᴡᴇᴇɴ Windsor and Truro used to be something of an expedition into the wilderness before the roads were paved. At about the midway point the dirt road emerged into a clearing and descended a steep hill and then up another on the far side, where it divided in two. To the left were two churches, one United, the other Anglican, St. Paul's. To the right the road continued on to Upper Rawdon, beyond which lay the busy Halifax to Truro highway.

I spent a summer at Rawdon, camping out in the rectory and inflicting my early attempts at preaching on the patient folk of the community and nearby settlements. The rectory was so little furnished it did not even have wallpaper. Just outside the church door was the grave of the daughter of my grandmother's sister and her husband, the Reverend Ted Parry, whom I knew in his old age. He used to say that Rawdon was the best parish he'd ever had. My mother had

an oil sketch of St. Paul's (left) painted by Robert Harris in 1912, when he spent a summer holiday there with his nephew, the Reverend Charles Harris.

St. Paul's Church, Rawdon, has Gothic style windows, but in its proportions and trim it is neo-Classical. It was built in 1845 just when Georgian was giving way to Gothic Revival in the Maritime provinces.

I shall never forget an experience I had one day that summer. I had taken a couple of days off, using my father's Morris Minor car to go down to Liscomb on the Eastern Shore to visit my mother's cousin, Father Walter Cotton, CR, who was living in the rectory there under a Rule he had written himself, attempting to start a new religious community. On my way back to spend a third night away with my parents in Windsor I passed through Rawdon, not intending to stop. However, just as I was passing churchwarden Charlie Moxon's house a terrible noise erupted under the floor of the car, forcing me to stop. I went into the house, where Mr. Moxon told me a parishioner had died suddenly and that he and others had been trying all day to get in touch with me. On examining the car I found that a small rock had become lodged in its chassis and that the vehicle had suffered no damage. Immediately I set out for the home of the deceased parishioner where I was able to offer comfort to his family and make arrangements for the funeral.

The fact that the rock flew up into the car in front of Charlie Moxon's house and not anywhere else on my long journey that day on rough roads prompted questions in my mind that I still ponder.

Ten: Great Village, Great Church

I N NOVA SCOTIA THE GOLDEN age of church building was coincident with the golden age of shipbuilding, and it was in seaside communities that some of the province's finest timber-built churches were erected by the same hands that built the ships. The ships are now long gone, but most of the churches remain. One such is Great Village's St. James's United (formerly Presbyterian) Church — surely one of the finest rural churches in the province. It was built in 1883 to plans drawn by architect J. Charles Dumaresq, 1840–1906, in a distinctive High Victorian Gothic style that might be described as an example of what architectural historian Eric Arthur called "picturesque eclecticism." Dumaresq (who more often employed a neo-Classical vocabulary, as for example in his St. John the Baptist Roman Catholic Church at nearby Springhill) based St. James's

in the Early English Gothic style, as is evident in his use of lancet windows and broad-spreading roofs in the building. But he enriched it by adding other elements as well, like the octagonal belfry that sits atop a square, buttressed tower, set beneath an eight-sided spire. Useful interior spaces flank the principal entrance in the base of the tower. Their exterior roofs, set lower in the front elevation than the main roofs of the nave, create an impression of size in what is, after all, only a moderately sized building. Unusually in a rural church built in the eighteen-eighties, St. James's has transepts and a basement hall, features that also contribute to its impression of large size. Around the main doorway there is some rich surface texturing, and the building is embraced by string courses with decorative roundels; but these features tend to be blanked out by the white paint that covers everything but the buttress caps and roof.

Photos by H.M. Scott Smith.

Eleven: First, Second...?

AFTER THE AMERICAN REBELLION SOME thirty-five hundred black Loyalists made their way to Nova Scotia. Some settled in the Tracadie area in the eastern mainland, but many of their descendants, lured by the prospect of jobs, moved into neighbouring Pictou County, settling mostly in New Glasgow when they found restrictions placed on where they could live in the nearby towns. But that did not mean that racial attitudes in New Glasgow were much different. Well into the twentieth century blacks were not welcome in restaurants, and in the local cinema, The Roseland, they were made to sit in the gallery rather than downstairs. About 1940 Carrie Best, the wife of railway porter Albert Best, challenged this rule together with her teenaged son Calbert, and they were both arrested. It happened again in 1946 when a black beautician from Halifax was arrested for sitting in the whites-only section of The Roseland. This time Carrie Best published her story — and others like it — in the *Clarion*, a newspaper she created that year out of a church bulletin. Carrie died aged ninety-seven in 2001, a member of the Order of Canada and the recipient of honorary degrees from St. Francis Xavier and King's College.

Calbert was one of my friends at King's College, and throughout his time there he lived in one of the single rooms on the top floor of the residence that normally were assigned to seniors in their last year. It was one time that racial segregation worked in his favour. In my three years at King's I never got to live in one of these coveted rooms. My roommate (white, of course) for two of these years was also from New Glasgow. Much of his later life, I understand, was spent in jail, while Cal went on to be the national president of the Civil Service Association of Canada and High Commissioner to Trinidad and Tobago.

Properly, this vignette ought to be illustrated by a photo of Second Baptist Church in New Glasgow, one of twenty African United Baptist churches in Nova Scotia, but it burned in 1985. Instead, here is an archival photo of the architecturally interesting First Baptist Church of New Glasgow, a fascinating blend of the Chateau and "Richardsonian Romanesque" styles, sub-species of the Queen Anne style dominant in house designs in the late Victorian/Edwardian era, adapted to church architecture.

Epilogue

THIS CHURCH-CRAWL (AS IT might be called in England, the ecclesiastical equivalent of a pub-crawl) has taken us through a number of buildings and several histories, and now it is time to pause and reflect on what we have seen and, perhaps, learned. As an Anglican, I have found the Roman Catholic, Orthodox, United, Presbyterian, Lutheran, and Baptist churches immensely interesting — each of them similar in different ways to my own — and if I have not penetrated as many obscure corners in them as I have in the Anglican fold, I apologize. I am sure they are there.

There are some churches I have not gotten around to, and again I must apologize: Pentecostals, Nazarenes, Bible Chapels, Seventh-day Adventists, Wesleyans, Jehovah's Witnesses, Latter-day Saints (both Reorganized and unreorganized), and more besides. An entire book could be written about the Reverend Perry Rockwood and the People's Church in Truro, a Nova Scotia phenomenon, but all the attention it receives in this one is a brief reference and a photograph.

But of course the fact that there are so many religious denominations raises questions about them. Did not Jesus pray that His followers all be one?[35] The three churches reflected in the still waters of Mahone Bay (actually, there are five in the village) are very pretty, but ought not there be but one church in a place the size of Mahone Bay? In our studies there, and in Lunenburg and a few other places like Clementsport and Crousetown, we found tales of ecclesiastical hubris and jostling for pre-eminence that not only reflect little credit upon the denominational protagonists, but that also have led to an oversupply of church buildings in Nova Scotia that could (and probably should) lead to the loss of many of them, as populations shift away from rural parts, and from city centres to their fringes.

But this is not just a matter of demographics. Some of the churches caught in the redundancy conundrum are of such architectural or historical merit that they ought not be lost, whatever their circumstances. And, of course, churches are best preserved if they are continued in the function for which they were built: as places for liturgy, and the offering of prayer and worship. It is therefore good to see churches preserved by secular bodies as museums, like the Barrington

Meeting House, being used as venues for ecumenical services. Others, like St. Patrick's in Sydney, are so full of exhibits that they can no longer be used for worship.

But one should also consider the possibility that a larger number of churches than necessary exists in Nova Scotia because God decided not to put all His eggs in one basket. If there were but one church and it proved inadequate to the divine requirements, its failure might thereby be isolated, and God's purposes fulfilled by others. After all, St. John the Baptist, in debate with the Pharisees, suggested that God could raise up "children to Abraham" from the stones by the side of the road if those who were Abraham's children by nature were unresponsive to their vocation.[36] At least, the multiplicity of denominations that sprang up in places where Protestantism was most successful, with doctrines that suggested that the true church of God is invisible and composed only of those predestined to salvation, or that lay believers can generate valid sacraments from within their own circle without the necessity of apostolic succession or episcopal ordination, would seem to be in accordance with Christ's suggestion. Yet He did pray that His church be one, and He did say that the "gates of Hell" would not prevail against it.[37]

But the multiplicity of churches has also a multiplicity of causes, other than doctrinal differences. Many of the churches have an important ethnic dimension, even some of the Catholic churches, as we saw in Whitney Pier. Perhaps that is the elusive model being sought by the modern ecumenical movement — a church that is Catholic, and yet not monolithic.

Nevertheless, the multiplication of churches in Nova Scotia seems very wasteful. The British policy in colonial days was to try gently to push or pull the Acadian, German, Swiss, Montbeliard, Mi'kmaq, and American communities towards the Church of England, as it was then by law established. But the lesson of the civil war in England, and of the many wars of religion that had been fought on the Continent, was that attempts on the part of the civil authority to impose unity of religion by force were bound to fail, and that toleration was an alternative preferable to ongoing religious strife and violence. If Nova Scotia communities, in contrast, say, to towns and villages in Quebec, have too many churches, it is because the Protestant understanding of the church accommodated more easily the diverse ethnic and religious mix of the Nova Scotia population than the Catholic understanding, so much a part of the fabric of Quebec, which envisaged a single homogenous community that offered but a single face to the sacred as it did to the secular.

Many of the Nova Scotia churches were built at a time when means of communication and transportation were very different from what they are now, when the pace of life was slower, and when there was less choice of activity and interest with which to occupy one's time. If the place of prayer and worship appears to have shrunk (like the length of sermons) in the lives of many people in recent years, it may be that it is not so much because of loss of faith as because of competing demands upon the time and attention of individuals. But this may still amount to the same thing, like the character Evelyn Waugh refers to, who lost his faith through inattention, like a man losing his umbrella in a railway carriage.

At the same time, there is no question but that Nova Scotians lavish great care and attention upon their church buildings. They remember them in their wills, they keep them clean and well painted and in good repair — often at considerable sacrifice.

Sometimes in the discharge of this stewardship they commit offences against "architectural correctness" — a tyranny perhaps comparable to political correctness, but nevertheless a requirement if good design is to prevail. The Anglican diocese of Nova Scotia, for example, has rules that provide excellent procedures for the protection of the architectural integrity of its buildings, but they are frequently ignored in practice. Unless the required sensitivity exists in the local congregation, the overseeing authority, if there is one, is unlikely to risk an uproar by intervening to correct the situation. After all, there are far more serious and fundamental sources of conflict in churches than disputes about whether or not to repair or discard a spire or slap on vinyl siding.

Photo courtesy of Acadia University.

Upper Canard Baptist Church; archival photo of 1907.

In preparing this book we found many churches throughout Nova Scotia locked. In a few urban churches in tourist areas, we found students hired for the summer as guides in buildings that were open for a few hours each day. The fires in Halifax and Lunenburg have made those responsible for churches very nervous. The great majority of Nova Scotia's churches are built of wood, and, of course, are highly combustible. Yet thirty to forty years ago, most rural churches remained unlocked during the day, as well as those in cities and towns. It is almost as if today the churches are under siege, outposts in an increasingly alien world of a Kingdom that its Founder said "is not from hence."[38]

Still, in every city and town and village throughout Nova Scotia, the churches are among the most noteworthy public buildings, and are attended by faithful and, in many cases, large congregations. They witness not only to the Gospel of Christ but also tell in their windows and on their walls of local folk and families and the lives they lived, often through many generations. Portraits of the priests and ministers that baptized them, taught them the Ten Commandments as children, married them as adults, comforted them in bereavement, stood by them and prayed for them in trouble, and laid them to rest at the end of their days to await the Last Day of all, look down from church walls all across Nova Scotia. In many churches there also hang on walls photographs of clergy with their congregations (I have included an early one — of the United Baptist congregation at Upper Canard in 1907), a reminder that the Church is people rather than buildings.

It is perhaps a necessary reminder for those who buy and read books such as this, which, on the face of it, might be thought to be about buildings, but which is mainly about people: the People of God in Nova Scotia.

Glossary of Terms

Aisle: Wings on the side of a church divided by piers from the main structure; often used instead of alley to refer to the passageway between the pews or seats in the nave, or main body, of a church.

Ambo: A stand, raised on two or more steps, for the reading of the Epistle and the Gospel. Usually there were two, one identical to the other, and stood on either side of the chancel. Popular in medieval Italy, they were later replaced by the lectern and the pulpit.

Apse: Semicircular or polygonal termination, usually of a chancel.

Arcade: A series of arches supported on pillars.

Baldacchino: A canopy, usually over an altar.

Baroque style: A style of architecture that developed out of the Classical tradition in the seventeenth and early eighteenth centuries, "characterized by exuberant decoration, expansive curvaceous forms, a sense of mass, a delight in large-scale sweeping vistas, and a preference for spatially complex compositions" (the *Penguin Dictionary of Architecture*).

Bay: A vertical division in the wall of a building marked by buttresses or pilasters, etc.

Bishop: From the Greek *episcopos*, meaning "an overseer."

Board and Batten: Vertical siding on an exterior wall with narrow strips covering the edges of adjoining boards.

Broach spire: A slender octagonal spire rising out of a squat pyramidal structure set on a square tower.

Buttress: A mass of masonry built at an angle to a wall as a support; on a wooden building usually an ornamental feature, although it may sheathe a diagonal supporting timber.

Cantoris and Decani: The two sides of a chancel or choir; originally, in a cathedral, the north side, where the cantor sat, and the south side, where the dean sat.

Capital: The head, or crowning feature, of a column.

Cathedral: A church in which the diocesan bishop has his cathedra, or chair.

Celebrant: The presiding sacred minister at the Eucharist.

Chancel: The limb of a church on the opposite side of the crossing from the nave.

Clerestory: The upper stage of the main walls of a church above the aisle roofs, usually pierced by windows.

Cornice: Any projecting ornamental moulding along the top of a building, wall, arch, etc.

Crypt: A basement.

Decorated style: Middle period in English Gothic architecture, in which the ogee, or S-shaped curve, is prominent in window tracery.

Diocese: An ecclesiastical territorial jurisdiction headed by a bishop; originally a unit of secular administration in the Roman Empire.

Dorsal: A curtain or other structure behind an altar.

Early English style: First period of English Gothic architecture, in which the pointed arch is first used, with narrow windows without tracery.

Elevation: Any external face of a building; also a two-dimensional drawing, without perspective, of one such face of a building.

Episcopal Peculiar: A church directly administered by the diocesan bishop.

Eucharist: Memorial of Himself commanded by Christ. The word is Greek, and means "Thanksgiving." It is also called the Mass and the Holy Communion.

Fleche: A slender spire, usually of wood, rising from the ridge of a roof; also called a spirelet.

Fresco: A method of painting on walls on a freshly laid ground of stucco or gypsum.

Geometric tracery: Window tracery in which circles or foliated shapes decorate the window head.

Groin: The edge formed where vaulting surfaces meet.

Hammerbeam: Horizontal bracket, usually projecting at the wall plate (top of a side wall), supported by braces and carrying arched braces and struts. Hammerbeams lessen the span and help reduce lateral pressures of the roof.

Helm roof: A roof with four inclined faces joined at the top, with a gable at the foot of each one.

Hood-mould: A projecting moulding above a doorway or window to throw off the rain. It is also called a dripstone or a label.

Lancet: A narrow window with a pointed arch.

Lectern: A book-stand from which a reading is made.

Liturgy: A Greek word meaning "work," used to describe the service of worship offered in church.

Mensa: Top surface of an altar table.

Narthex: A vestibule at the main entrance to the nave of a church.

Nave: From the Latin *navis*, or "ship," the main limb of a church west of the crossing, usually accommodating the congregation.

Oculus: A round window.

Palladian: A style of neo-Classical architecture derived from the buildings and publications of Andrea Palladio, the most influential of Italian architects.

Pediment: A low-pitched gable above a portico, doorway, or window.

Perpendicular style: The third period in English Gothic architecture, in which large windows and straight vertical and horizontal lines are predominant.

Pilaster: A shallow column or element applied to, but projecting only slightly from, the wall.

Presbytery: A house occupied by a priest; a body of priests, or presbyters, resident in a specified area.

Priest: Shortened form of presbyter, a Greek word meaning "elder." Normally used today to translate the Greek *hieros* and the Latin *sacerdos*.

Pyramidal spire: A spire with four sides.

Quatrefoil: A foil is a leaf-shaped curve, or lobe, made by the cusping of a circle in Gothic tracery. The cusp is the projecting point between the lobes. A quatrefoil, then, is a circle with four cusps and four foils.

Quoin: Dressed stones at the corners of buildings, usually laid so that long and short ends alternate.

Reredos: A wall or screen or other ornamental structure rising behind an altar.

Retable: A shelf or ledge above the back of an altar.

Rib vault: A framework of diagonal arched ribs connecting the cells of the roof surface.

Sacristy: The room in a church in which the vestments and sacred vessels are kept.

Sanctuary: That part of a church interior containing the altar, usually at the eastern end of the chancel; in some Protestant ecclesiastical traditions the entire interior area of the church is referred to as the sanctuary.

Specifications: Detailed instructions prepared by the architect for the builder.

Spire: A tall pyramidal, polygonal, or conical structure rising above a tower and coming to a point.

Steeple: The tower and the spire taken together.

Stringcourse: A continuous, projecting, horizontal band set in the surface of a wall and usually moulded.

Tracery: Ornamental intersecting work in the head, or top, of a window.

Transept: Transverse arms of a cruciform, or cross-shaped, church.

Triforium: An arcaded wall passage facing the nave above the arcade of piers and arches at floor level, and below the clerestory windows.

Tudor arch: A flattened, four-centred, Gothic arch, popular in England in the fifteenth and sixteenth centuries.

Umbrage: A shadowed entry; a deep or recessed space designed to shelter persons arriving at a door.

Vestry: Room in a church building in which ministers or choir vest for the service.

Bibliography

Fleming, John, Hugh Honour, and Nikolaus Pevsner. *A Dictionary of Architecture*. Middlesex: Penguin, 1972.

Wallace, Arthur W. *An Album of Drawings of Early Buildings in Nova Scotia*. Heritage Trust of Nova Scotia and The Nova Scotia Museum, 1976.

DeCoste, John A. and Twila Robar-DeCoste. *The Little Wren Church: A History of St. Mary's Anglican Church*. Hantsport, Nova Scotia: Lancelot Press, 1990.

Duffus, Allan, Edward MacFarlane, Elizabeth Pacey, George Rogers. *Thy Dwellings Fair: Churches of Nova Scotia 1750–1830*. Hantsport, Nova Scotia: Lancelot Press, 1982.

Pacey, Elizabeth, George Rogers and Allan Duffus. *More Stately Mansions: Churches of Nova Scotia 1830–1910*. Hantsport, Nova Scotia: Lancelot Press, 1983.

Fingard, Judith. *The Anglican Design in Colonial Nova Scotia, 1783–1816*. London: S.P.C.K., 1972.

Cuthbertson, Brian. *The First Bishop*. Halifax: Waegwoltic Press, 1987.

Cameron, Silver Donald. *The Education of Everett Richardson: The Nova Scotia Fishermen's Strike 1970–71*.

Brownless, Basil. *The Story of Lunenburg's Most Historic Church: The 250-year history of St. John's Anglican Church*.

Two Hundred and Fifty Years Young: Our Diocesan Story 1710–1960.

Tuck, Robert C. *Gothic Dreams: The Life and Times of a Canadian Architect, William Critchlow Harris, 1854–1913*. Toronto: Dundurn Press, 1978.

Tuck, Robert C. *Gothic Dreams: The Architecture of William Critchlow Harris, 1854–1913*. Charlottetown: Confederation Centre of the Arts, 1993.

Celebrating our Heritage: a History of St. James Presbyterian Church, Truro, N.S. The Worship Committee of St. James Presbyterian Church, Truro, N.S., 2001.

Ned Harris's Letters From Mahone Bay. Ed. Robert C. Tuck. Charlottetown: Maplewood Books, 2001.

Raddall, Thomas H. *Halifax: Warden of the North*. Toronto: McClelland & Stewart Ltd., 1948.

Emsley, Sarah Baxter. *St. Paul's in the Grand Parade 1749–1999*. Halifax: Formac Ltd., 1999.

McAleer, J. Philip. *A Pictorial History of St. Paul's Anglican Church, Halifax, Nova Scotia*. Halifax: Resource Centre Publications, 1993.

Parish histories of St. George's Greek Orthodox Church, Halifax, Fort Massey United Church, Halifax, and St. Matthew's United Church, Halifax.

www.stfx.ca/people/lstanley/History/architects.htm

www.stmatts.ns.ca

Sources and Acknowledgements

THE IDEA OF THIS BOOK, as well as a good deal of practical assistance in the implementation of it, I owe to architect H.M. Scott Smith, author of *The Historic Churches of Prince Edward Island*, published by Boston Mills Press in 1986. Many individuals have been helpful in many ways, and I wish especially to thank Kevin Rice, Dr. Gerald Boudreau, Sister Julie d'Amour, FMA, the Reverend Ewen Moase, the Reverend Peter Rafuse, the Reverend Dr. Robert Crouse, Miss Susan Harris, Professor Henry Roper, the Reverend Dr. Ross Bartlett, the Reverend Daniel Boudreau, the Reverend Tom MacNeil, Canon Gary Thorne, the Reverend Theodore Efthimiadis, the Reverend Trent Cleveland-Thompson, Bishop Vincent Waterman, Patricia Townsend, Stephanie Veinot, Lynda Shalagan, Garry Shutlak, Eric Croft, James Burchill, Elaine LeBlanc, the Reverend Edward and Mrs. Tuck, and their son, Graham Tuck, a very busy digital reimager who took most of the photographs in this book, and his wife, Angela, who spared him to go with me on fast journeys up and down the length and breadth of the seaside province during the summer of 2003.

Photo Credits

Graham Tuck: photos of subjects in Clermont, Auburn, Halifax, Yarmouth, St. Bernard, Clementsport, Middleton, Cornwallis, Granville Centre, Barrington, Mahone Bay, Crousetown, Springhill, Truro, Sydney Mines, North Sydney, Baddeck, Jordan Falls, Windsor, Whitney Pier, Bear River, and Antigonish.

Art Gallery of Nova Scotia: photo of the Serres painting.

Confederation Centre of the Arts Gallery & Museum: photos of the Arichat and Springhill churches.

College Ste-Anne: three archival photos of Church Point and St. Bernard churches.

Fr. Daniel Boudreau: a Chapter 13 photo.

Acadia University Library: Upper Canard Church photo. First Baptist, New Glasgo, photo.

Adam Corelli: photo of Robert Tuck.

H.M. Scott Smith: St. George's Round Church photo, page 42, St. James's Church, Great Village photos, page 136.

Tom Kavanaugh: Chapter 13 photographs.

Edward A. Jordan: St. John's Church, Lunenburg, photographs.

Notes

1. "For one man who felt within the joy of Rowland Taylor at the prospect of the stake, there were thousands who felt the shuddering dread of Cranmer. The triumphant cry of Latimer could reach hearts only as bold as his own; but the sad pathos of the Primate's humiliation and repentance struck chords of sympathy and pity in the hearts of all …" Green, J.R. *A Short History of the English People*. New York: Harper's, 1889. 368.

2. First patent dated August 9, 1788.
   Second patent dated August 13, 1788.

3. Letters by the Reverend John Breynton to the Society for the Propagation of the Gospel in December 1755, December 1760, and January 1762. Also in sketches by Richard Short — purser on HMS *Prince of Orange*, 1759–61 — using a Camera Obscura. These sketches were later used by Dominique Serres to create paintings of Halifax, including the 1759 painting reproduced in this chapter.

4. *250 Years Young: Our Diocesan Story 1710–1960.* 17. This history of the diocese of Nova Scotia has no identifiable author.

5. www.stmatts.ns.ca

6. ibid

7. Fingard, Judith. *The Anglican Design in Loyalist Nova Scotia*. Published in 1972 by the Society for the Propagation of the Gospel, London.

8. From the parish history "The Little Wren Church."

9. ibid

10. Johnson, *Global Odyssey*.

11. Duffus, MacFarlane, Pacey, and Rogers, *Thy Dwellings Fair*.

12. ibid

13. Bell, *The Foreign Protestants and the Settlement of Nova Scotia*.

14. St. George's parish minutes, MG4, Vol. 317 #1.

15. Bell, 622.

16. St. George's parish minutes, Vol. 2 #29.

17. St. George's parish minutes, Vol. 2 #31.

18. Letter from Bishop Charles Inglis to Christian Brehm et al. of St. George's. St. George's parish minutes, MG4, Vol. 323 #3b.

19. St. George's parish minutes #4.

20 Brownless. *The Story of Lunenburg's Most Historic Church.*

21 Sinclair, D.M. *Fort Massey Church, Halifax, Nova Scotia 1871 – 1971 A Century of Witness.* 14.

22 Tuck, Robert. *Gothic Dreams.* 178

23 Ibid. 226.

24 *Gothic Dreams.* 175.

25 Unfortunately, the stone work in the new front elevation facing Tower Road had to be rebuilt in 2003, only twenty-four years after its construction in 1979. According to Cathedral Property Warden Ray Carter, "it was shoddily done when initially installed (low bidder?) and was about to fail catastrophically." It had been built only one year after the publication by Dundurn Press in 1978 of my biography of William C. Harris, in which I described in detail the troubled construction history to that point of All Saints' Cathedral (*Gothic Dreams,* pp. 175–200).

26 Nobbs-Thompson Report, 1929.

27 Letter from Goodhue to Archbishop Worrell.

28 Nobbs-Thompson Report, 1929.

29 collections.ic.gc.ca/parole/ie/creditsgerald.htm

30 collections.ic.gc.ca/archaeology

31 *The Gathering Storm.*

32 collections.ic.gc.ca/co-op

33 *Celebrating our Heritage: A History of St. James's Presbyterian Church, Truro, N.S.* 100.

34 *History First Baptist Church Halifax.*

35 St. John 17:20–21.

36 St. Matthew 3:9.

37 St. Matthew 16:18.

38 St. John 18:36.

About the Author

Photo by Adam Corelli.

Robert Tuck was born in Bridgewater, Nova Scotia, raised in Mahone Bay and the Annapolis Valley, educated at King's School, Windsor, Dalhousie and King's universities in Halifax, and St. Michael's College, Llandaff, Wales. After stints as a newpaper reporter and school teacher he trained for the Anglican priesthood and served parishes in Wales, Nova Scotia, and Prince Edward Island, where he is a canon of St. Peter's Cathedral. *Churches of Nova Scotia* is his seventh book (two are collections of cartoons) and second for Dundurn Press.

In 1959 he married Catherine Elizabeth Greene of Vancouver; they have two children: Dr. Elizabeth Eayrs and troubadour Alan Tuck.

About the Photographer

Photo by Adam Corelli.

Graham Tuck lived his early life in Parrsboro and Chester, Nova Scotia, and started his career as a commercial photographer in Vancouver, after receiving a First Class Honors BFA in photography from the University of Victoria. Through his photography he began using computers, first to edit, then to create images.

Currently, Graham is a freelance graphic artist in Halifax specializing in computer graphics and interactive content for television and the web.

His wife is the former Angela Murphy.